Tears
and
Healing

Tears
and
Healing

The journey to the light
after an abusive relationship

by

Richard Skerritt
(previously, Richard, 21CP)

Dalkeith Press
Kennett Square, Pennsylvania

Published in 2005 by
Dalkeith Press
873 East Baltimore Pike #742
Kennett Square, PA 19348 USA

Library of Congress Control Number: 2003098469

Softcover Edition
ISBN: 978-1-933369-01-9

Also available in Hardcover Edition
    ISBN: 978-1-933369-00-0
And PDF e-book Edition:
    ISBN: 978-1-933369-02-7

Cover Image used under license from Corbis.

Sixth Printing, December 2012

Notice

This book documents the personal experience and perspectives of the author.

The author is not a psychologist, psychiatrist, counselor, or therapist.

While this book may contribute to your understanding of your situation, it is not a substitute for professional help. If you are in distress, please seek help from someone trained to help you.

If you are in an abusive situation and in danger of physical harm, seek safe shelter. Most US locations have domestic violence hotlines listed in the phone book, or call information and ask for domestic violence help.

If you have thoughts of ending your own life, call your therapist, counselor, doctor, or emergency help number immediately. These people are trained to help you.

Contents

Introduction

So you married someone with big problems?

Or you chose another significant relationship with someone suffering from alcoholism, or a personality disorder like borderline personality disorder (BPD). Perhaps your spouse started out seeming fine or even wonderful and only showed problems later. Maybe you're just beginning to realize that your partner is abusive and hurtful to you. Perhaps you already know that your partner suffers from alcoholism or borderline personality disorder, or has been diagnosed with some other illness. Perhaps you grew up in a neglectful or abusive home, or perhaps you're the victim of a brutal and punishing divorce system.

Whether it is one of these or some other difficulty that brings you to read this, you're most likely suffering. This book might help you with that. It is a compilation of the many insights I have gained as I have healed from my own experiences in a marriage deprived me of emotional support and ultimately became abusive. One thing is for sure: it is not idle chatter. While many of the individual

1

topics here will challenge your assumptions or make you think about things in a different way, they're all reflections of real challenges that I have faced. They may be good or not so good; they may help you or they may not. But at least they are authentic.

My experience was highly colored by an understanding of BPD. It is arguable whether my wife really has now or did have BPD. If you read the diagnostic definition of BPD, you may find the same uncertainty concerning your partner. The reality is that the characteristic behaviors of BPD are found in varying degrees in many seriously unhealthy people. So I encourage you not to be distracted by my references to BPD, because what is really important is the unhealthy behavior and not how we label or classify it.

I use the word *non* a lot. In communities concerned with alcoholism, this refers to the relative or partner of the alcoholic--the "non"-alcoholic. In the context of BPD, it refers to the partner or relative of the person who has BPD or traits of BPD. In general, it refers to group of people in situations that are probably quite similar to yours. In other words, when you read *non*, think of *yourself*.

I Offer a Perspective on Recovery

Through this book, I share the wisdom I have accumulated as I have progressed through my own recovery from a sick marriage that became emotionally brutal to me. It is one view of a **path** starting from the emptiness, hurt and confusion of an unhealthy relationship and leading to understanding, some amount of serenity and greater fulfillment as a human being. It's not a cookbook, and it's certainly not everything you need to know. I've organized the presentation in chapters, but keep in mind that most of the sections within each chapter were written separately to stand on their own.

Recovery

Recovery is a word with roots in addiction - alcoholism and drug addiction - and refers to the personal and spiritual healing process that leads addicts to heal their wounds and find sober, straight, fulfilling lives.

Nons have a recovery process to work, too. We often don't realize this when we first start our healing journey and find out we are not crazy, and not alone. Our significant others (SOs) are very sick people, and we tend to focus on them. But we are sick, too. We are damaged by abuse, neglect and distortion. We are victims of brainwashing that impairs our ability to see right and wrong. And we are often isolated from contact with the people who care about us and can help us heal.

And we have other issues, too, that we brought into the relationship. Most of these center around not having strong enough personal boundaries: the knowledge and will to say "No! Not with me!" These issues are often called codependence. To heal and move on, we must address the damage done by the relationship *and* the codependent issues we started with.

3

I hope this book will help you in your personal journey.

Who Am I? Non-Guy? Famous Philosopher?Richard, 21CP?

I am, first of all, a recovering former non. I was married to a woman with serious emotional problems for 18 years, 18 of which were painful. At that point the relationship ended, at my insistence. We have two children: who were eight and 12 at that time.

I am an engineer by training and worked 22 years with a large company. Today I write, publish, operate my own information technology, teach, and consult. Outside of my work, I have been a loving and involved father, I sometimes do some nice cabinet making, and I'm active in sports.

When I began writing on the internet, I chose the pseudonym Non-Guy. I was then, and remained until well after my wife moved out, fearful that she would find what I have written and know it was about her. I didn't even want to use my real first name. She could be a vicious, emotionally brutal person. I don't volunteer to go there.

After some months living safely by myself, the hyper-vigilance – the constant fear and watching out for her – faded. I no longer really worry that she'll find all this. If she does, it will be her problem. Once I really felt separated from her, I decided to retire the Non-Guy pseudonym. It served me well, but after all the healing I've done, I no longer like to think of myself as a non-BP, or non-alcoholic, or non-anything. I am just me, and that would be, well, a famous 21st century philosopher. For some time I used the email id famous21centphil. You all will figure out after reading a few pages that this really means a 21-cent philosopher. But keep the pennies. Hey, I'm a generous, famous philosopher.

When *Tears and Healing* was first published, I chose the pen name Richard, 21CP. As I wrote more, I selected a new pen name, Richard Skerritt, a name with a basis in my family's origins in England and Lebanon. Today, *Tears and Healing* is printed under this pen name.

As a non, I was a major contributor to the online support groups (p. 32) on WelcomeToOz and BPD411Intro. It is primarily as a list member that I wrote the initial versions of the sections that make up this book. Many have been adapted from email posts that addressed a particular situation and were sent to those lists. This is the nature of support lists, where we talk to one another as we learn and grow by sharing. I had posted some of these in my support groups so many times I realized it was time to formalize their presentation.

Take What You Like, Leave the Rest

I am not a therapist. I am not a psychiatrist. I am not your mommy or your next husband. I am just a guy, who happens - no, used - to be a non. People seem to benefit from what I have to say, so I offer it here. Please use what you can, and leave the rest. I never mean to judge you or tell you what to do, even if my writing may sound that way. Only you can decide what is important and what is right for you.

Oh. About NEC...

You'll see references to NEC and NECW throughout the book. (If you come across abbreviations, you can check the glossary starting on p. 177.) My former wife, like many who have BP behaviors, was never diagnosed with BPD, and never will be. In fact, by the official diagnostic manual of the American Psychiatric Association, the <u>Diagnostic and Statistical Manual of Mental Disorders IV</u> (DSM-IV) definition, she did not have BPD. Yet all the patterns of thought, feeling, and behavior match with BPD. This is another painful and frustrating side of this disease. My then-wife vehemently denied she had BPD - "Not Even Close!" in her words. From this came the acronym NEC, which symbolizes both the denial that is part of the disease, and the confusion in the mental health community about BPD.

The key is not diagnosis. Clinicians rarely see the behavior they need to make a proper diagnosis anyway, because it is hidden from them. What counts is the behavior in the family, understanding what motivates it, and how to deal with it. Ultimately, we all face the question of whether our significant others (SOs) will heal. What we learn, as we wonder, is that *we* won't heal until we decide to heal ourselves.

Fare Thee Well

I wish you well. It is a long journey, my friend. But it is filled with the joy of learning, the pain of letting go, and the fulfillment of finding, and learning to love, yourself.

Godspeed.

Richard

Tears and Healing

Chapter 1
My Story

You might think that a book intended to help you deal with your situation would not be about me. Seems strange, doesn't it? But, what I've found very consistently is that those in the online communities who have used these writings find great value in hearing my own experiences.

I guess all this famous philosophizing gives the initial impression that I must somehow be different from the thousands of nons who have sought help from my experience. But the truth is the truth: I have had to work through all the same challenges that every non faces. Fortunately, mine have not been as difficult as those that some face, but I have had my share.

So, here is a brief rundown of my life experiences, at least as they seem to relate to my learning and healing as a non.

My Life

I don't want to spend too much time on the mundane. But there are a few aspects of my existence that bear on my relationship, so I'll explore them briefly.

Childhood: I am very thankful that I grew up in a loving home. I can honestly say that I never doubted my parents. They were there for me, and they cared for me and about me. I know that this makes me different from most nons.

Parental Models: My parents' relationship with one another was neither antagonistic nor particularly loving. But there is one dynamic that I adopted. There was an undercurrent of my mother controlling my father through mild anger and contempt; and compliance on my father's part. I think this pattern was the primary model for my future relationship. Without it, I doubt that I would have tolerated the behavior I experienced.

I've also come to realize that my mother was emotionally distant. She worked to be a good mother, and she tended responsibly to our home and to our needs. But she was not emotionally close or warm. My father was, but my mother was not. My mother grew up in a home where she felt unloved by her mother, who she said rarely interacted with her. This pattern of being somewhat emotionally distant is reflected in the kind of women I have been automatically attracted to.

Obligation: My childhood family was principled. From this I learned a very strong sense of obligation. This ultimately was a source of great pain for me. I was taught to comply with others' expectations at the expense of my own well being. I don't believe this was intentional on my parents' part. Nevertheless, it was very strong. It caused me to stay in an unhealthy situation far too long, which resulted in serious emotional harm to me.

Work: I was fortunate to get only one job offer when I finished school. It brought me to the company I still work for. My work has been the foundation around which my personal growth has centered. It was at work that I first realized that I needed to make changes in my life. It was a colleague who ignited my dormant spirit by offering me a copy of the *Tao te Ching* (p 163). Work has been the testing ground for me as I have learned to live more and more "with the way" rather than fighting. I don't know why, but I have been blessed with a job that has allowed me to range widely outside my work, and still has rewarded me well. Some things are not understandable, but we can still be grateful for these acts of grace in our lives.

My Relationship

Here is a short review of my relationship with my soon-to-be ex-wife:

I met my wife when I was 19. I was immediately attracted to her good looks and bright mind.

Tears and Healing

From the time I met my wife, until we were married seven years later, I never seriously wanted to be with another woman. But that's not to say that I was with my wife. I started out as a closet boyfriend - a hidden relationship while she continued publicly to see her existing boyfriend. At the end of the school year, I disappeared from her consciousness. She simply stopped acknowledging my existence.

A couple of years later, she reappeared. Now I was no longer second in her hierarchy, I was third or worse. This went on for a year or so. Finally I said "no more." At my insistence, the relationship ended.

But fear not. She reappeared yet again. It was here that I asserted the only real boundary I ever set with her until our divorce. I said "me and me only." She agreed.

A couple of years later, after both of us finished our studies, we were married. We quickly bought a home, at her urging. It was then that the BP facade started to crack. I started feeling like I was under constant criticism. Our relationship suffered. Within months her criticism was coupled with complaints that I didn't love her enough. She was right – it was hard to love her when I felt constantly put down. Yet neither of us ever considered ending the relationship. For both of us, this just wasn't an option.

About one year into our marriage, we moved at my employer's request. My wife quickly found a job. However she became very depressed. She was

Chapter 1
My Story

not resting at night, she was consumed with her work most of the time, and the relationship suffered even more.

We moved back after about two years. Now my wife was anxious to have a baby. I frankly never thought very hard about having children one way or the other, and I complied with her wishes. Our first daughter was born.

After about one year, my wife chose to stop working. At the same time, she started infertility treatment. She became depressed and almost constantly dysphoric – displaying strong inappropriate emotions, usually anger. Lacking proper boundaries, I accepted her behavior and did my best to "cope" with it. I started experiencing stress-related physical problems.

Her depression became severe, yet she did not seek help. I can remember her telling me during this time that I needed psychiatric help. I was emotionally battered and lost. I could not even see that she desperately needed mental health care. She spent most evenings immobile in a recliner in our room.

Our second daughter was born and shortly after, my wife, in desperation, went to a depression screening. They nearly hospitalized her on the spot. She began therapy and medication, and she improved some. But her therapist was the first in a long line to suggest that she divorce me. Her problems continued, varying in severity, but anger, contempt and criticism were a daily experience for me.

About the time our second daughter was born, I began my own recovery - without really realizing it. I began developing interests and rejecting the dominance of her behavior. The relationship continued to be miserable, but I was now finding some fulfillment outside. I was participating in sports outside the house that soon became an energizing and fulfilling endeavor, one that allowed me to meet and interact with many people. I was now on my way.

By this time, I had lived with seven years of constant anger, contempt and criticism. Our marriage was little more than co-parenting. In August, after a short burst of her feeling well, my wife became severely depressed, and essentially abandoned me with the girls while she poured all her effort into her studies. Her quack psychiatrist put her on tons of medication. She took it, and more, and drank as well.

She was a zombie. I thought she was *just* mentally ill. By year-end I thought she might die. I was caring for our children almost alone, and I began preparing myself emotionally for her death. I now know she was well into addictive disease at that time. Then, she had a migraine and overdosed herself on some combination of pills and alcohol. Shortly after, I insisted she back off her meds and she improved. But the severity of her problems had caused me to take a big step back from her in commitment. I already really hated the way she treated me. Losing commitment made this worse.

Chapter 1
My Story

In the next year, I was becoming very consciously unhappy with my life situation. I was doing well in my work, my sports activity was great and I was enjoying it immensely, and I was growing spiritually and interpersonally. Of course my wife hated all these changes in me, and continued to hate them until we separated. The Disney movie *Mulan* had just come out, and I was introduced to the song "Reflection" - a song about not following your true self in life. Ouch. This song was a kind of a catalyst for me.

Eventually, my unconscious mind decided that enough was enough. This is not a comfortable thing for me to talk about, but I will. I was around a young woman often. She was a clone of my wife in many ways, including the mental health and behavior problems, something I now understand made me likely to be attracted to her. I fell powerfully in love with her. I never had a special relationship with her; and I dealt with these feelings by trying to ignore them. This was painful. I wrestled with the idea of leaving my wife, but I felt obligated to stay. I really thought she would die if I left her.

Around this time, my wife overdosed again. This time we nearly hospitalized her. However, she objected strongly and so we found her a new, codependent therapist instead. I had completely lost any hope of having a relationship with her. But the new therapist seemed to help her. She seemed to be much like her "old self." Looking back, I realize this was a desperate attempt to reverse the years of ugly treatment and keep me.

Underneath, she was regressing and becoming more and more ill as her alcoholism, still hidden from me, worsened.

Finally, demonstrating my fine coping skills, I awkwardly approached my young friend. She declined to be involved with me. In fact, she never spoke to me again. I now suspect that she "split me out of existence," a subconscious coping reaction in which she avoiding dealing with painful memories by simply not acknowledging that I existed. Even though I did nothing to cause her such pain, I must have triggered memories that were painful. At the time I did not understand. It was very painful.

At this point, I was distraught, and I came to my wife and told her briefly what was happening. She was very supportive - for about two hours. After that, intense rages began, and continued at intervals for many months after. Among the prices I paid for this: she insisted I break all my social ties and isolate myself from the new friends I had made. This was a brutal price for something that had happened only within my feelings. But I was distraught, and I agreed.

Within a few months, her alcoholism, still hidden, was taking over. She was going really crazy. I did not know - I thought she was *just* mentally ill. I discovered BPD at this time. Her behavior clearly matched BPD patterns. Within a couple of months she was near death.

She finally admitted she was abusing alcohol and unable to stop. She went into outpatient alcohol

Chapter 1
My Story

rehab then. She made some good progress, but continued to relapse every three weeks or so, becoming more suicidal on each relapse. By June she was again very near death. I called 911 and the police came and sent her involuntarily to the ER. She was very near committing suicide when she went into an inpatient rehab.

She came out much improved, and has stayed sober and done well with the girls since then. However, her periodic rages continued, and she continued to attack virtually every aspect of me and my life, including my parenting. She HATED that I had contact with anyone, even Al-Anon. She pressed me to go to couple's counseling. We went to one session. That night, and the next morning, she went into a violent rage, preventing me from leaving the room, screaming every hateful thing she could conjure.

This episode convinced me I could not go on with her. I began making plans for divorce. She was now on her best behavior, again trying to fix the situation, but I did not care. Within two months I had chosen a lawyer, and had consulted a therapist about the impact on the children.

Finally, I told her that I would not go on with her. I said I would not leave the house or the children, and asked to settle the divorce and custody while still living together, and then both move to new homes. About two weeks later she raged again, in front of our younger daughter, and threatened me. I did not know that what she said was criminal and that I could call 911, but the next day I went to the police and was told her statements were "terroristic threats" and I could complain. I chose to leave it with a report, in case it repeated. It did not, but the character assassination continued in the context of the divorce discussions.

My wife progressed through denial, anger, anger, anger and anger. I consistently asked for the girls to live alternating one week at a time with each of us. After months of verbal abuse she agreed to this. In May we settled all the terms for alternating week custody. One clause that the mediator suggested, and I then insisted on, was counseling for the children. My wife was terribly emotionally distressed by all this, and felt that I had forced her to do something that was not best for the children. But she signed nonetheless.

She was very distressed just from being in the house with me. She had already moved down the hall to the guest room since I wouldn't "just get out." She felt that she could not go on living in the same house until we settled the divorce. She found a lovely home – expensive -- and signed a lease. When the girls were out of school, we told them of the divorce and the living arrangements.

Within a week, my wife moved to her new home. The girls easily adapted to changing homes. They clearly want to be with both parents. They come into each of their homes as if it is their own. They have not shown any signs of serious stress. I made arrangements and we started them in counseling. The therapist, a PhD psychologist, found no indication of any adjustment problems, found both girls well adjusted, and discharged them after about eight visits. They do, of course, have experiences that may surface later and cause distress. But for now, they are doing great.

My former wife continues to do better with each month. At this writing, after two years of foot-dragging, it looks like she will settle out of court. Her emotional stability is increasing greatly. I believe that giving her problems back to her through divorce was probably the best thing I could have done for her.

I'm still too poor to run the air conditioning, and in fact I'm pretty house-poor overall. I'm holding my breath, hoping for time to heal all financial wounds. Meanwhile, I've done well with the challenge of half-time single parenting and trying to figure out how to be a half time single guy. Still lots to do there.

My Divorce Process

I want to share some aspects of my own divorce process. I think my outcome has been a lot better than many non husbands achieve, and so there might be some ideas that could be adapted for others.

I like the lawyers term "innocent and injured," which is how I perceive myself in this marriage (never mind that she blames me for everything, a characteristic of emotionally unhealthy people.)

Research First

I began by researching the effect of divorce on the children. I spent the next month getting a therapist to advise me on this. I also reflected very deeply on whether to seek to full custody. After all, I was in fear in my own home. How could I go away and leave my children in the care of someone I was afraid of?

I learned that the most damage to children comes from losing contact with a parent. Even when the parent with less time stays in contact with the children, they still tend to feel that they have lost that parent. Since their mom was abusive to me and not them, I felt that I could not fairly deprive them of her caring. Moreover, since she had done little directly to the children, I felt it a virtual impossibility for me to get a court to award custody to me. I decided that I should not seek to keep them from her. I resolved to move forward in a way that would keep both of us actively parenting them. Their mom, while still unhealthy in her interactions with me, does well with them.

I also learned that the children's stress is much reduced when there are no unknowns, and the parents are in command and in control. Telling the children that big changes are coming without letting them know what those changes are is very difficult for them. Therefore, I resolved to stay together in the house with my wife until the custody schedule was settled, new living arrangements were set, and the children could be told exactly where and when and with whom they would live.

Chapter 1
My Story

This turned out to be a tall order. However, my wife, who even at her worst was situationally competent as a mom, confirmed these concepts with her therapist, and apparently felt compelled to comply.

I spent the next month searching for an attorney. I interviewed three, and hired one that had worked as a rehab counselor, knew what BPD was, and was very tuned into my concerns about abandonment issues in divorce. I also used this time to research finances: child support, alimony, property division, income tax effects, real estate prices and values. Basically I tried to rough out what I thought the financial picture would look like after divorce to make sure I could live with it. And since I wanted our children to have a good home with their mom, she also needed to be able to manage.

During this time I also contemplated what I felt was right materially. I felt that I had done nothing wrong, and should not be forced to leave my home. I also felt that I should not be penalized financially to the extent that it seriously changed my standard of living. This too, is a tall order in a divorce with her not working. But she has not one but two masters degrees, and could certainly earn a very reasonable living given some startup time. I resolved that this burden should be on her and not me. I did not know how much this could be accomplished.

Breaking the News

Shortly before I was ready to tell her, she said that she was going to see a lawyer to "protect herself." It turns out she had found the biggest, nastiest litigator in the county: someone who never settles, but fights to the end. I let her go without comment. The next day I told her that I wanted a divorce, that I wanted her to mediate custody and that I wanted alternating weeks 50/50 custody, and that I wanted her to mediate support and property distribution. Custody is the first issue to be settled, both legally and from the children's standpoint.

Shortly after, I was treated to a "terroristic threat" in which she said she wanted me dead and had thought of many ways to do this; would get me fired (presumably while still alive), etc. I filed a police report but did not ask to have her charged.

After a couple of visits with her therapist, she said that her therapist said alternating weeks would be good for her and the children, and she was ready to agree to it. I said let's get a mediator and start. She said she wasn't ready.

Ah, The Distortions..

By late January a new phase began - an ongoing series of ugly conversations alleging that I was a pervert and a pedophile and she could not leave the children in my care. Of course, she would say this and then go out for three hours and leave the children in my care. Hmmm… This went on for two months, and she finally agreed to mediate but only with a mediator of HER choosing. None of

Chapter 1
My Story

the mediators my attorney recommended would do - she had to have one specific attorney mediator. I checked and said this was not someone I would choose to work with. I said she was known to jam agreements down people's throats and this was not good for either of us. But she insisted.

We went to a two hour mediation in which my wife presented me as an unfit father whom she was afraid to leave in care of our children. The mediator, a woman, seemed not at all concerned that my wife had been drunk, suicidal and raging not eight months before. She told me I was likely to feed the children chocolate cake for breakfast. I left the mediation without speaking to my wife and began preparing to fight a custody battle. I did not speak to her for two weeks. The verbal attacks stopped.

Finally she emailed me, asking me to choose a mediator. I agreed, and decided on a PhD psychologist who has experience with addicts in early recovery. This was a good choice. Over about eight hours of mediation, my wife went from "no way" to agreeing to almost everything I asked. Concessions that she asked for that I wrote up she later dismissed. The mediator told my attorney she was concerned my wife was too fragile to mediate. Luckily, her nefarious husband was secretly planning a custody arrangement that was in the children's interest. In my wife's words, "You got everything you wanted." Well, I got what I felt was right for the children.

Toward the end, I realized that for the children's well being, one parent should stay in our home. It isn't cheap, and this was a problem. She said "No way." She would never leave me in the home with the children. At this point, she was near breaking under the emotional strain. Even with a therapist, a psychiatrist, an AA sponsor, and many, many AA friends and supporters, she was barely hanging together. I simply refused to say I would agree to any path at that time.

However, she was becoming extremely distressed at home. She asked countless times "Won't you PLEASE GET OUT?!!" I answered "This is my home/bedroom/bed. If you don't like being here with me, you can leave." This wasn't easy, but I had been practicing for nearly a year already, and I hung tough. She could no longer stand being in the same room/bed and had moved down the hall, taking about everything she could pick up, including some of the furniture. This was not enough, however, and she found being in the house with me very distressing. She also felt she was fine away from me, and I was the cause of her distress and bad behavior.

She signed the custody agreement, and shortly after, asked me for money so she could sign a lease on a house. It was very expensive, but she insisted it was the right choice. Right after school ended, she signed the lease; we told the children of the divorce, the custody arrangement, and their mom's new home. They adapted to it without difficulty. There was no uncertainty, and they saw their new home the same day we told them of the divorce.

Chapter 1
My Story

Their mom moved out in July, a helpless victim of a nefarious husband who was selfishly keeping the house and half the contents of the house (and mortgage and utility payments, by the way.)

I made a support and property offer shortly after. I did a lot of work, using our actual expenses, tax calculations, etc., to make a detailed plan showing how she could pay her reasonable bills on that support plus reasonable pay, which allowed her time to find a permanent job. It was a fairly considerate offer. Although I was not generous, it showed that she would be very comfortable once she got a permanent job. The offer was rejected and she filed with the court for child support and temporary alimony. I prepared my arguments with my attorney for the conference to set the initial support.

At the conference, the officer gathered all the pay stubs, and we argued about my wife's income, and finally we did indeed get into this person's head the actual average of her last six months income. Then we muddled through mine, and then, lo and behold, when my attorney said, "She has gift income," the officer included it. This was a big help for me, and it is true. Her mother had made annual gifts to both of us continued to give this to my wife.

Anyway, her computer clicks away and surprise! Out comes almost exactly what I offered her!!! Take that you selfish attorney! The child support was $10 different from my offer. The temporary alimony was $195 higher. And that was based on her having less income than I assumed. So it turns out that not only am I a stellar author, but I also wield a pretty mean financial planning spreadsheet.

The bottom line is that I will NOT be eating peanut butter sandwiches for dinner. I will be eating them for lunch, though, and I will need the extra calories for all the extra housework I'll be doing and the physical strain of living without air conditioning (not in the budget). But at least I can keep my evil study- the room she demonized because I actually communicated with other people via my computer there. I just have to sweat a little more in the summer. I haven't figured out whether I can afford to heat the place in the winter - I guess it depends on how cold it gets.

Conclusions

1 - Divorce is complicated and merits a lot of planning. If you can do this, it really helps.

2 - Reflecting deeply on what is right (not what you want, but what is right) helps to set goals that are achievable.

3 - By sticking tight to your home and your children, you can keep your reasonable claim to these strong.

4 - Custody can be mediated with a BP, but you have be able to be a grownup in the face of raging and abuse. I managed, but barely. Given the choice again, I would definitely mediate. The only thing to lose was time and money and the abuse.

Chapter 1
My Story

5 - I can't take credit for this, but as a working father I can say that the support guidelines in Pennsylvania, for 50/50 custody, are not horrendous. While I have to pay alimony and child support, they are not much higher than the cost of supporting the same people in my home. When she gets a real job, I expect that it will cost me less in support than the actual cost. This isn't fun, but it means the situation is bearable.

6 - Getting divorced stinks. But being married to a raging spouse is way worse.

7 - By taking real care to protect the children from uncertainty and fears that their parents are not in control, and setting custody so that both parents still parent, the injury to the children can be greatly reduced. I think my girls both feel that this situation is better than what we had when great tension existed between their mom and me.

8 - Change is scary, and hard (see the section on Fear, p 145.) It's tiring and it makes you cry. But it's positive growth and sets the stage for a non to evolve into a former non, and have a peaceful, happy life. The damage to the children need not be traumatic, and when one spouse is really sick, the children may well feel better after separation.

Tears and Healing

Chapter 2
Contacting Reality

Starting Recovery: The First Steps

If you're like most nons, when you first face up to dealing with your partner's problems, and what all this has done to you, you are confused and overwhelmed with feelings. You've lost touch with what is right and wrong, with what is acceptable and not acceptable. And you are probably fighting an amazing buildup of fear, hurt, frustration, deprivation, and loneliness.

Although there is a lot of learning and growing ahead, in the beginning, the key task is to get your head screwed back on as straight as can be, and to get your emotions to a point where you can deal with them and process some other things, too.

1. **Work on the confusion**. The first thing you need to address is your confusion about what is right/wrong, good/bad. It's characteristic for BPs and troubled partners to distort their SOs' (Significant Others') realities to support their

illness. And since they isolate us, we lose the stabilizing input of others. So you need **input**. If your partner has BPD, or traits of that disease, the book *Stop Walking on Eggshells* (p. 171) is the best grounding. Hopefully you have it already and have started to put the pieces together.

However, you'll probably find that you still doubt that the things you're experiencing are *really* the same as you're reading about. The email support lists (p. 32) are great for letting you see examples of other's experiences, so that you can compare them to yours. And the similarities are scary. It's funny, but it seems that all seriously troubled people have the same playbook they work from. But it's going to take a while before you start to realize that, "Oh, that really is *his* fear he's projecting onto me!"

And my favorite recommendation: find some healthy people around you and **talk to them** -- family, friends, coworkers, neighbors, whatever you've got. They will help you. You'll be surprised how supportive people can be. They know you, and they will vouch for your reality. They can reassure you in a way that others can't. You might be surprised how many people around you have had their own problems, and can be very understanding of yours.

Now with this input you need to **output**. Start writing. And don't shortchange it. Support lists are a great place to do it, but you can keep it private if you prefer, or share with just a close person. But the important thing is to **write down what you think**. While you may reflect a lot about things as

you read, writing is a synthetic process that forces
you to put the thoughts together in a complete
way. You can think of it as making a persuasive
case to others, but the real benefit is that you'll
convince yourself. And ultimately, you are the
only person that needs to be convinced.

Later you'll read a section on brainwashing (p. 57)
that helped me to really grasp how badly my wife
was treating me. By writing it, I made the case for
me to push through the denial my wife had put on
me and to believe how bad it really was.

2. **Work on the emotions**. They are real. They
demand your attention, and you can't shortchange
them. You are hurt. You are neglected. You are
abused and demeaned. These feelings are real, and
you have them for a reason: they're the right
feelings! The problem is that you don't feel that
they're the right feelings. I'll say more about this
later, when I talk about memory and what we have
to do to heal.

As a first step, you need to *express your feelings,*
and find people who will *validate* and *support*
them. You can say them, write them, scream them,
or carve them in your SO's back, but spit them
out. The support lists (p. 32) are really good for
this, but there are other avenues. For example,
whether your SO has a drinking or drug problem
or not, you can attend Al-Anon (p.35) or Nar-
Anon meetings and you'll get loads of listening
and validation. And therapy (p. 33) is yet another
avenue for this kind of validation.

After you work on this for a while - I'd figure three to six months if you're like me - VOILA! You will begin to find a new strength, and a new perspective on yourself. And you'll probably be ready to start making some other really significant changes. Chances are, if you're reading this, you need to.

Support Lists

Support lists are a powerful force you can tap for your personal growth.

Support lists are groups in which the members share by email. When a member wants to share, he/she sends an email to the list address. It's sent to a list server, which is a fast mail server computer. The list server relays the message by modifying the title to include the list name, and forwards the message as an email to everyone on the list.

Now, I'm not the list police, and I'm not a cheerleader. I don't know about all the lists that are out there. I'll just point you to the lists I personally know about and can vouch for. Things change with time, so use your judgment.

The lists I personally know of and have participated in are:

WelcomeToOz - a general non support list. For info:
http://groups.yahoo.com/group/welcometooz

WTOStaying - a related list that welcomes those who want to stay in their BP relationship, or still have value for their BPSO even if they can't stay.
http://groups.yahoo.com/group/wtostaying

WTODivorcing - which focuses on the issues in divorcing a BP spouse
http://groups.yahoo.com/group/wtodivorcing

WTOTransition- which focuses on the transition away from living with a BP partner
http://groups.yahoo.com/group/wtotransition

BPD411Intro - for all aspects of non relationships
http://groups.yahoo.com/group/bpd411intro

Therapy

I hate to say this, because my own experiences with therapists have not always been good, but most nons need to consider talk therapy. You may not realize the scope of the damage that your relationship has caused. Plus, many nons come from childhood backgrounds that, just by themselves, probably call for therapy.

Therapy can do two things for you.

1. It gives you access to someone who, hopefully, has broad technical knowledge about what might be going on inside you. Things that may seem puzzling or just painful to you may fit into a pattern that the therapist can see. And once seen, it becomes something you can deal with.

(Well, actually, much of what you'll read here fits that general description. But again, I'm NO therapist.)

2. It provides a safe, confidential person you can share with. And if you haven't seen it elsewhere on these pages, I'll say again that *sharing with other human beings is essential to your recovery*.

You'll probably pick up from some pages here that my experience with therapists has included some very bad ones. But you should remember a couple of things about that. First, these interactions were with my wife's therapists, who are obligated to her and not me. Second, I haven't tried hard to make it better.

Therapy *is* very helpful for many people who hurt or are confused. I encourage you to seek it out and try it in good faith.

Group List Therapy

I also strongly encourage you to participate in an email support list (p. 32). These groups can be wonderful. You'll find intelligent, caring people like you, and you'll get many of the same benefits you would get from professional therapy. You'll learn so much about yourself, the disease, and how others have coped. You'll have a chance to share in an anonymous, caring group that can help you feel like you're not alone in your difficult cares and concerns. It is free and the benefits can be great.

Al-Anon

Al-Anon is a healing tool that you should consider, especially if you are feeling a strong need for face-to-face support with real people.

Al-Anon is a passive program of spiritual growth. It has teachings on acceptance, detaching, letting go, caring for yourself, and so on. It offers a community of people meeting face-to-face who can share your burdens and offer support. Don't worry if you don't think you have an alcoholic in your life. You don't need one. Just go. You'll be welcomed and your stories will be similar to many others.

Why do I call it passive? Because Al-Anon is a strictly managed program that limits its writings and discussions to its own controlled content, and it does not lead. It does not advocate approaches. It simply presents twelve very general steps, and the experiences of others, and you do what you can with it. And this is a problem for many people. For example, what I write in this book may be right or wrong for you, but I have an opinion. I have suggestions and encourage specific actions to help you. This is leading. It may be right or wrong for you, but it is a lead you can follow if you choose.

Al-Anon, in contrast, never does this. And while people do find their way in life with help from Al-Anon, the program seems to frequently leave people confused and frustrated. The only guidance offered is to just keep coming. And this is not right for everyone.

Higher Powers

Al-Anon helps people deal with living with somebody who's really emotionally sick. While there are twelve steps in the Al-Anon program, much of the program hinges on Step One, which is to admit you are powerless and you cannot control another person. You can't make them stop drinking, stop being BP, get a job, stop picking their nose, etc, etc. Although this is difficult, it will greatly help to free you from a burden that really isn't yours. You can then focus your energy on you and finding the right path for you with or without your troubled partner.

Now I don't structure my beliefs in line with organized religion, but I do believe in a higher order. And I have to say that, in the state my life was in during the traumatic changes I went through, I couldn't be in control of my life even if I wanted to, because there were forces larger than me at work. So I slowly realized that I needed to "Let go and let God."

A shortcoming of Al-Anon's approach is the tilt toward giving up control. The initial plunge into 12-steps is focused on giving up the illusion of control and accepting a higher power's will. Perhaps this place of total uncertainty has some value, but it is frightening, and I'm not sure that it's realistic. We are, after all, independent beings, and we do make choices from day to day. So a more comfortable place might be accepting that we cannot control others, but we can control ourselves, and we can shape our future once we accept that others are outside our control.

But My SO Isn't an Alcoholic

The "requirement" for participating is "a problem of alcoholism in a friend or relative." Surely your grandmother's cousin's daughter was an alcoholic, or someone at work. That'll do. Seriously, it IS all the same. And there is no entrance exam for Al-Anon - you don't ever have to say a word. But when you hear the stories that are told, some are pure alcoholism, but lots and lots are just like our lives. We could all fit in perfectly. And we know that there is a high overlap between the people with additions like alcoholism and people suffering from personality disorders.

What's more, I can't imagine any Al-Anon group would ever discourage anyone from attending who sincerely wanted help. You would be welcome in any group.

Al-Anon Stories

During the most difficult time when my wife was so sick, before I could sort out what to do, I read the short (one page or so) summaries written by those who have used Al-Anon to heal and move on (In All Our Affairs, p 163.). A few of these were very helpful for me, because they validated the way I felt about how I had been treated. The two that really stood out for me dealt with an adult coping with childhood sexual abuse, and someone who had been unfaithful to their abusive, alcoholic spouse. In both cases the individuals were led to accept their feelings as real and realistic, and to self-forgiveness and self-honor. Since my abusive wife was desperately trying to demean me and destroy my self-esteem, these stories were especially relevant.

There is a side to these stories that bears mentioning. The overwhelming majority recount decisions to stay in a marriage that was unhealthy and deprived the non of the love and support that we all need, and must find through our spouses. In this sense, Al-Anon seems to be a vehicle for stabilizing and sustaining people in situations that are arguably unhealthy for them. As you'll see later in the book, I feel that healthy people cannot remain in situations that deprive them of intimate love and support. Yet Al-Anon seems to, by example, point to this outcome as a desirable one. So I would advise caution in the use of these stories.

Final Disappointment

Ultimately, I found Al-Anon group meetings don't give me the support I needed. I come from a "fairly" healthy family, and I was never mistreated or neglected as a child.

I found it very hard to relate to Al-Anon members who, at 40-50 years old, are still struggling with the way their father treated them or how they never had the things in life other kids did. Their growth process, though no less valid, is far too different from mine.

Chapter 2
Contacting Reality

I have, in fact, a fairly well developed spirituality. In Peck's (p. 165) paradigm, I'm well into the final stage 4. And it has helped me tremendously in my work if not my family. I combine my own spiritual base with the shared experiences on the support lists, and with the many readings I've undertaken. This has been a solid combination that has really allowed me to grow in my own way. It is this synthesis of these many sources of support and knowledge that I offer in this book.

In the end I chose to spend my time in reading, reflecting, and writing. At one time I thought there may come a time when my needs might change, and I might chose to start attending again. But after several years, I can honestly say that I think I've gained all I can from Al-Anon, and my personal growth will take place in other ways.

Finding Al-Anon

The best way to locate Al-Anon meetings in your area is using the phone book. In my area, when you call the number, you get a choice to hear a recording of the meeting schedules or to leave a message asking to speak to someone. Well, Al-Anon isn't exactly the federal government, but it does work and the groups do meet.

You can also find out more about Al-Anon on their web site:

http://www.al-anon-alateen.org/

and by searching for Al-Anon in any search engine. If you use a plus sign (+) immediately before the city and state you live in, it will limit results to just pages having those names on them. However, such information on the web may not be provided directly by Al-Anon and may be less accurate than calling the Al-Anon number in the phone book.

Online Chat

Online chat offers another way for you share thoughts and feelings in a group setting. Chat is simply exchanging one-line messages in real-time with one or more other people. AOL instant messenger is a chat program. For non-BP recovery, you might be able to chat within a structured chat room, where you can feel confident that the others share similar experiences.

Chat can be good for times when you are dealing with a very difficult situation: a major rage or emotional violence, or acting out behavior. It's like a conference call, but typed. I have never been big on chat, but the chat rooms have helped me out on days when I was really hurting.

Many nons in chosen relationships are isolated. Isolation is a big part of the BP's arsenal of abuse. Chat is a connection with others that some nons are able to use without disclosing it to their SOs. It can be a lifeline for some in tough situations.

Formal Chat Rooms: I am not aware of a formal chat room, devoted to non's issues and moderated to keep the dialog safe and on-topic, that's available now. They have existed recently. Check

the non resource sites given later (p. 171) to see if
any have been set up.

Individual Chat: As you get to know people from
the support lists or the formal chat rooms, you
may choose to chat privately.

Tears and Healing

Chapter 3
The Disease and You

You are living with an experience that is painful and confusing. It might be tempting to think that all this is the result of your partner's disease. But in reality you are experiencing the *interplay* of you and your partner. It is only by understanding how you and your partner function, and how you interact, that you can begin to really judge what is happening. With that understanding comes the ability to make informed choices that will improve your well being and happiness.

This chapter is written in the context of borderline personality disorder (BPD). You may see that many of the disordered behaviors described here apply to other problems as well. That's because no one disorder has a monopoly on any unhealthy behavior, and also because many times people have more than one problem at the same time. Again, take what works for you and let the rest slide by.

There are good books on BPD and the behaviors and feelings that go with it. I especially recommend *Stop Walking on Eggshells* (SWOE, see p. 171), which covers both the BP and non. What I offer here are some slightly different perspectives that might add to your understanding.

Onions and Scrambled Eggs

Many nons feel that there is a "good core" in their BPSOs (significant others with BP or boderline personality disorder,) and that, much like an onion, they can somehow peel the layers of the disorder away, revealing this beautiful diamond core. Of course, most all of us live (or did) with behavior that varies all over the map from violent to adorable. Is it just a layer?

If you're going to make good decisions, it's important to understand what you live with. First, let's look at BPs who are sick, in denial, and don't accept responsibility. This isn't a mood. This isn't a passing state. I'll say more about healing later, but to begin, we need to keep in mind that BPs are disordered and will stay that way until they accept responsibility for themselves The idea of a shimmering diamond is enticing, but is it there?

One analogy I have used around this issue is:

"My H is really a good, law-abiding person. It's just that every once in a while he robs a bank. But really, deep down inside, he is a good, law abiding person."

Chapter 3
The Disease and You

The only way I can make sense of this kind of alternating behavior is to back up from it. In my mind, the basic truth is:

Good, law-abiding people don't rob banks. When you see someone rob a bank, you know they are not a law abiding person.

I would apply this to a definition of a loving person: A loving person does not demean, derogate, hit, kick, spit on, or rage at other people. When you see these behaviors, you know that you are not seeing a loving person.

A disordered person is just that: disordered. There is no gem of personality inside the disorder. This is why they are called personality disorders - because they disorder the entire structure of the person. Living with a disordered person and thinking there is a sparkling diamond waiting for us to uncover is unrealistic. We can never peel this onion. A BP is more like a scrambled egg. The tendency to be loving and good is intertwined with the compulsion to be hurtful. There is not some diamond inside, covered by a crust. The whole person is disordered - scrambled, if you will. You get it all together, or you get nothing. You might read the Parable of the Tree (p. 70).

Projected diamonds: And what is it that makes up this scrambled mess? Is it a diamond? Is it the precious person we imagine? Well, only healing will tell, but it's not likely. The "ideal" persona that we sometimes see in our SOs is not an expression of their true self. It is a facade, held up to avoid rejection. Surely that cannot represent their core. And like everyone, we project our own wishes and desires onto others, including our SOs. "Oh, isn't she sweet?" we coo at a toddler, even though she may be far from it. It is what we value and wish to see. We do this with our SOs, too. I talk about this a little in On Changing Values (p. 117). Our perceptions of our SOs are distorted by both their ideal facades and our own projected desires.

Not our onion: More importantly, even if this were an onion, it is not our onion to peel. Only the disordered person can choose to do that. It is not our responsibility to do that; it is not within our power to do that. If we are focused on "helping" our BPSO, we are in the wrong place. We need to be focused on helping ourselves. It is up to our SOs to choose to change.

BPs and Healing

In the section Memory Shapes Us (p. 124), I talk about a model for how abuse affects us. One part of that model is the life energy that I believe we all possess, which I call our spirit. This is the wellspring of all our motivation and the source of the energy that drives our lives. Everyone has a spirit, and that includes BPs. Indeed, BPs seem to have a tremendous life energy drive - it's just that it finds expression in unhealthy and hurtful ways.

The wonderful aspect of our spirit is its phenomenal power to heal us. When we can open ourselves to its energy and its messages, it can empower and enable us to achieve amazing things. Even healing a personality disorder.

But to make this happen, the BP must assume responsibility for his life and his behavior. Once someone accepts that he is responsible for the choices he makes and the way he behaves, he can then begin to tap that life energy and use it for healing. But it is like a catch 22. A primary defense for BPs is denial and blame shifting. So before healing can start, denial must stop. But this means a big part of the disease must stop before healing can begin. What a mess! It really takes a leap of faith to get started.

And when healing takes place, a new person must be melded from what is present and what is learned in the healing process. Old coping habits must be dropped; new ones substituted. Patterns of thought must change. Yes, the spirit within that person can emerge, and can find expression as a complete person, but the shape of that newly formed diamond is unknown until it is formed. It is a rebirth and reformation process the outcome of which can't be known beforehand.

Staying Realistic

My point in saying this is not that we must all abandon everyone who is not well, but we need to be realistic about what we are living with. Loving people don't abuse. Abusers are not loving people. And no matter how much we love our SOs, as long as they remain in denial, our love will not bring out some precious hidden personality. Only our troubled partners can make the choice to take responsibility for their own lives and strive to be well. Those that choose to make life changes can overcome their compulsion to be harmful and evolve a new and unknown personality. Unfortunately, few BPs will make that choice.

A stable, loving partner can help reduce the compulsion to be harmful, but doesn't generally bring forth a loving relationship. Therapy and medication can help, but generally only to reduce the intensity and frequency of the harm. If the BP does not make the gut-wrenching commitment to take responsibility, things will never be normal.

The diamond is an illusion, painted by them to overcome the problems they know they have, reinforced by our projected needs. In my case, it was a fantasy inspired by outward appearance and my projection of an idealized "inner spirit" (the diamond) onto her.

Regardless of whether our intention is to stay, be ambivalent, or go, it is important to get a realistic perspective as soon in OUR lives as we can, and understand the key difference between denial and assumption of responsibility, so that we can better deal with what confronts us.

Abandonment/Vulnerability

The flip-flop of emotions in a BP relationship can be devastating. This is usually called abandonment/ engulfment. It's described well in Stop Walking on Eggshells (p. 171)

Chapter 3
The Disease and You

I've been split into oblivion by two women I've gotten close to, and I struggled to understand the dynamic. Both women ended their relationship with me by simply acting as if I didn't exist, presumably because they had connected me with some prior, very painful experience. It's a coping mechanism that protects them from anything or anyone that reminds them of memories that are too painful to deal with.

In trying to understand these experiences, I took a little different view. I've been influenced by an interesting book: *Struggle for... Intimacy* by Woititz (p 163), which deals with the behavior of Adult Children of Alcoholics (ACOA) in intimate relationships.

Abandonment: BPs, ACOAs, and other unlucky souls *were* abandoned as children. Not that they were left on the steps of an orphanage - that would have been much preferable. These people were abandoned *up close and personal*. When they needed love and support from their parents, their parents were right there to NOT give it to them. Moreover, they were told, over and over, implicitly and explicitly, that they were *despicable people* and that the terrible problems in their families were *all their fault*. They emerge from childhood feeling that they are terribly faulty people and that no one will ever be there for them. To protect themselves from the pain of this belief, they put up a mask of very proper and attractive behavior so that others won't see how awful they are.

49

So into their adult lives you come, attracted (so they think) by this false facade. They don't realize that you actually see their flaws. They are terrified that you will see through the facade and discover what an awful person they are. Once you see this, CERTAINLY you will abandon them just like their parents did. They struggle to make the mask perfect, but it can't be done. At some point, some error, some tiny flaw (trigger) becomes evident.

Well, the game's up; you now know how faulty they are. All you have to do is not fall over yourself reassuring them, and that's proof positive that you're outta there. They're going to freak out and all kinds of strange behavior will emerge.

One way they might react is projection: "There seems to be a problem here. It can't possibly be me. Therefore it must be you." And since you have a problem bad enough that you would abandon her over it, it looks pretty bad as your problem, too. You're gonna catch it for that.

Or, you may be hoovered (sucked back in, á la the vacuum cleaner) with all their might, trying to put that facade back in place and make things right. Or they may go to great lengths to get you to reaffirm your devotion to them, to the point of threatening suicide.

Vulnerability: Well, here I take a little different spin on things form the standard "engulfment" idea. I find it makes more sense to think of this in terms of vulnerability. Let's explore the childhood experience again. Here you have a child who needed emotional support. She opened herself up emotionally to her parents to receive this support. Instead she received emotional or physical attacks. She has learned that to stay safe, she must not expose her vulnerability to anyone else.

Of course, everyone wants intimate emotional support. And as an adult, she may eventually give in to this desire and start to open herself to you. She wants loving intimacy. But her childhood experiences force her to be on high alert for attack. After all, this is all she's ever known.

Unknowingly, you rub you nose the wrong way, or do something else that triggers her connection to painful memories. Well, her parents always did that. To her, this feels like a sure sign that you are secretly planning to attack.

Your ruse is up. Just as you thought you were getting close to her, you had to go and rub your nose the wrong way and spoil everything. She sees through you now. You are just like her parents, and emotions take over. Her fear is overwhelming, and causes her to attack back, or run. Maybe both. She may be so frightened by being vulnerable to you that she may turn you into the evil torturers that she had to live with as a child. It's not that she *thinks* you're like them. She's not thinking at all. The emotions are in control. As I like to say: **emotion overwhelms cognition**.

Your tiny action (trigger) was enough to make you fit the pattern. Her fears were unleashed from inside, and you are now a terrifying attacker. You might even be split right out of existence - simply become a non-entity. After all, that will at least make her safe.

So I like to think of it as abandonment/ vulnerability. Her self-loathing leads her to be sure you'll want to abandon her as soon as you see through her. Her experience of being attacked as a child means she will sense an impending attack when she makes herself vulnerable to you, and she will push you away to stay safe.

Don't leave me; you're terrible - the two edges of the BP sword.

Mental Short Circuits

A lot of people, in trying to understand rages or dysphoric episodes, will talk about thoughts, thinking or what is going through his/her mind. So let me illustrate with an experience I had with things going through my mind. I wrote this somewhere in the midst of my separation and divorce:

Yesterday and today I am very angry - not exploding, but very deeply aggrieved. I'm finding that I am very angry with drivers who drive slowly, traffic lights that are red, elevators that won't go fast enough.... There is a thought at the end of this reaction: "That SOB can't find his gas pedal," "This stupid elevator works like poop." But getting to that thought, there was no thought. The thought arises directly from emotion. I am frustrated, I am angry. Something frustrates my intent, and bingo! Thoughts appear - Irrational, counter-productive thoughts.

Chapter 3
The Disease and You

Now I'm not especially crazy, so I think this is insightful. Even in a "normal" person, strong emotion can lead to irrational, disconnected thoughts of great intensity. Now imagine the kind of emotional pain our SOs are in. Think about what kind of thoughts and intensity that must generate. It really becomes more understandable as you see the mechanics in a normal personality, and then add the intensity of a BPD personality.

When we've been verbally abused in a rage, we tend to respond, "She thinks I'm a pedophile ax murderer." But really, she *feels* so intensely, the emotions engender a thought of the same intensity. But she doesn't really "think" that about me. There's no reason, logic, or memory behind it. And considering how much pain they're in, we're lucky that's all they think.

So when our BPSOs (or whatever flavor you have of SO with a lot of emotional pain) are hurting, and they express thoughts about us, it's.... guess what... do you have it?...

Not about us.

It's not about us. It's not about them. It's not about anything except how much they hurt at that moment. They aren't "thinking" at all. Their "thoughts" are not thoughts at all. Rather, they are expressions erupting straight out of emotion; without logic, reason, or experience to support them.

Magical Stuff

Mirroring is when someone takes on the characteristics she believes we desire: she *mirrors* back to us what she sees we want.

I wrote the following early on in my own recovery:

Well, sometimes we wonder how we ever got into such a painful relationship. Many of us think we would never do such a foolish thing again. But the reality is not that simple.

BPs are magical people. They have powers that ordinary people will never have. And they are beautiful, intelligent, sensitive, insightful people. They have the power to short-circuit our brains and reach right for our hearts. These people move us in ways we always dreamed of and always hoped for. They fill us with feelings more powerful than we could ever have imagined.

If you took all the hurt in my life from everyone else, added it up, and multiplied by a million, it would still be less than the hurt I have suffered in my relationship with my wife (and she's not even BP! Not even close!) Yet, when despair for my relationship overcame me, my heart reached out - not to some nice healthy, divorcee my own age, who could love and cherish me - but to a sad, hurting girl just like my wife - complete with all the same problems.

No, I would never choose to be in a relationship like this again. But I just might do it anyway. So don't be too hard on yourself. Magic is powerful stuff.

Now, since I wrote that, I've had a chance to take a little better care of myself. Specifically, I stopped trying to accommodate myself and my feelings to a partner who was, practically speaking, intent on destroying me, at least emotionally. This has helped me a lot to get some closure on these intense attractions. At this point I haven't stepped into another relationship, but I think that when I do, I'll be steering clear of the warning signs that signal unhealthy attraction. All this comes out of my understanding that is covered later in the next chapter on finding yourself, and in the following chapter on love.

The Cusp of the Cycle

Our BPSOs' emotions tend to move through repetitive cycles. Some parts of the cycle can be particularly difficult for a non. If anything, BPs are unstable. They carry tremendous emotional tension with them. Innocuous triggers can unleash this tension. Moreover, AA has taught me that the stage can be set by simple stress on the person: HALT - being hungry, angry, lonely, or tired (and I would add PMS). My NECW is very prone to trigger when she is overtired, which she is a lot.

Typically, this emotional tension drops via the expression of the extreme moods and behaviors. I don't know if it's cathartic, or just exhausting. It certainly is hard on us nons. But after a while, the emotional storm will pass, and she will return to a calmer, more reasonable state.

Most of us have been through some fearful abuse at the hands of our BPSOs. This is hard. This is painful. And it leads to denial. Especially when they are able to get themselves together and function with a more normal level of emotion and behavior. There's really no helping it. Sometimes on the support lists you'll find members warning others about expecting too much when things are quiet.

But it's not a logical thing. It happens at a lower level. It is, in effect, our minds' way of protecting us from painful thoughts. Our minds simply refuse to retain the conscious images of the rages, dysphoria, and abuse. This is called dissociation. Since we don't vividly recall these, we tend to let our conscious thoughts follow. This is denial.

But, when the BP's emotions cycle back, whether it's a cycle or an eruption triggered by something, the denial runs smack into reality, and it's like hitting a brick wall. And it hurts. It feels traumatic, and it is. Because we've been in denial, we have trouble accepting what is happening. This makes it even more painful. And this, my friend, is the cusp of the cycle.

Later, under Constancy of Perspective, I'll talk a little more about working to stay connected during all phases of your BPSO's emotions. Just do your best to use YOUR emotional control to remember that she's in a lot of pain, and bad as it is, it's the best she can do.

Hopefully this gives you some comfort or some guidance in managing these emotional swings. There's not much to chuckle about in this part of the cycle.

Brainwashing -
An unsent Letter to my NECW

As part of my struggle to know where reality starts
and insanity stops, I wrote this letter to my wife.
No, I didn't send it to her. It would only have
triggered an angry response, and would never have
been forgiven. But I needed to do this to really see
the true extent of what was happening to me.

Dear NECW,

Today I am going to write to you about how you
are destroying my self-esteem. I'm going to use a
description of brainwashing from p. 63 of *Stop
Walking on Eggshells* (p. 171). So let me show
you how you are doing this to me:

- **Isolate the victim**: This one is clear. You
  have insisted that I can only talk to a
  therapist about my life. Then when I've
  tried to do this, you've told me you can't
  deal with this, and implicitly threatened to
  lose control and attack me even further if I
  had my own therapist. When I talk to
  someone at work, you attack me, and tell
  me I could have talked to my father, your
  mother, my brother, my friend. When I
  talk to my father, you accuse me of
  destroying trust in the relationship. In
  short, you insist that I isolate myself from
  everyone else in my life.

- **Expose them to consistent messages**:
  Over and over again, you tell me how I am

sick, how I will not take blame for our problems, how I never talk to you, never touch you, never respond when you "beg" me to change. You continue to attack me for dressing, acting, choosing cars and telephones in ways you don't want. You're not asking for change. You're not asking for anything. You're telling me you think I'm worthless and expressing unbounded contempt for me.

- **Add some form of abuse**: Your rages are abuse of the first order. And contrary to your assertions, these aren't new. They've only become more frequent and more intense. They are violent, deliberately hurtful attacks. They serve no purpose except to demoralize me. When you are not raging, you are acting out quietly: calling me at work dysphoric, accusing me of not being alone; getting me in a room or on the phone and not letting go of me even though no purpose is served. This is painful and abusive.

- **Get the person to doubt what they know**: This one is one you're getting better at. Now that your therapists have had a look at me, you're perfectly positioned to bombard with me "credible" assertions about how awful I am. You consistently tell me what you say your therapist said about me - always bad. I know these are distortions, based on what you say, but over and over you use this tactic, and it creates doubt. Why does everyone in the world think well of me but you and your therapists?

- **Keep them on their toes**: This is your best. You are always unpredictable. Anything can change your mood from stable to threatened. When threatened, you become accusing, critical, and often attack me. I never know what is going to happen when I answer my phone, what you are going to do when you walk into the study, who will be standing in the kitchen when I come in.

- Wear them down: see all of the above.

So you see, you are intent on destroying my self-esteem - brainwashing me to think badly of myself - and you work tirelessly toward that end. And I deserve better than that.

Tears and Healing

Chapter 4
Detaching and Finding Yourself

An insidious and really nasty thing happens to
nons who stay in relationships after they turn ugly:
we lose ourselves. We devote so much of our
energy, and direct so many of our choices, to
trying to make the situation better that we lose
track of what we are about as people. It happens
slowly and we don't realize what's happening. But
one day most of us realize that we almost
completely lost what we are as a person.

This chapter contains some of my insights from
the process of rediscovering me.

On Finding Yourself

There is a lot to say about this process of figuring
things out. There's the problem of understanding
what it is that seems to control the person you've
chosen to be with. And there's figuring out exactly
how you got to be where you are, why it seems to
hurt so much, and what happened earlier in your
life that led to it all. But, when all is said and

done, the real challenge in this is to figure out who you are.

I don't mean your name, or your occupation, or even your religion or what kind of God you believe in. Ultimately, it comes down to connecting with that inner you: that down-deep fundamental foundation of what makes you a human being. Now, everybody sees this a little differently, but this is about connecting with your highest authority, bypassing the should's and the must's and getting really down to what defines what you are.

Seeking Yourself

When times are good, we are happy with what we are and where we are, and we don't really need to push into hard questions. But when life puts us in a place where we wonder why we are suffering, why we are where we are, and we find ourselves totally confused about what to do to restore some balance in our lives, then we have got to look deeper. And ultimately, what we are looking for is *truth*.

It would be good if you could jump on the Internet, do a Google search for truth, jump to the vendor with the lowest price, and order some for next day delivery. No such luck. Truth is hard to come by. And the reason you can't order it online is that only you can define it. And the reason you need to seek yourself is that the definition ultimately resides *within* you.

Chapter 4
Detaching and Finding Yourself

Now, I always struggle with this deep stuff. People have different beliefs and frameworks, and I don't want to insult or alienate anyone. I believe, for what it's worth, that we are all playing by the same rule book, no matter what we call it or whether we read it from left to right or right to left. So let me try.

I think, unless you've been down this road before, that you are going to start with someone else's answer to the question, "Who am I?" If you're a Christian, then you are probably going to start with scripture. If you're more like me, then you're going to start with something philosophical/ religious, like Peck's book (p. 165), or who knows what else might click for you to get you going. What this will do is give you something to chew on, something that isn't the right answer for you, because your answer will be unlike anyone else's, but is in the right ball park. It's ok if it has some aspects that just aren't right, even 180 degrees off your course, because it'll still give you something to think about. Some of the other sections in this book might help, too, like On Seeking Permission (p. 143), What Happened to Me? (p. 115), or Tears and Healing (p. 137).

What you are looking for is some certainty that "I know what to do." And I don't think you'll find it in your head. I think you find it in your belly. It really doesn't matter what you call it. For those with strong belief in God, you might call it **God's will.** If you're more ecumenical (and I had to look that word up, even though I **felt** that it would fit, I wasn't sure **in my head)**, then you may call it

finding your **inner voice** or you **inner truth**.
Whatever you call it, I believe you will only find
that insight by inviting it. You must find a certain
level of peace or silence within yourself, and you
must be **willing to hear** the message you will
receive. And it really will come like a message,
seemingly from outside of your own awareness.

To make this happen, you are going to have to get
humble. If you pray, you are going to have to do
some serious praying—but not just the asking kind
of praying. You're going to have to do the kind
where you ask and then you wait for the answer,
where your question is put forth in a quiet, safe
place and you patiently listen for the answer to
come to you. When it comes, if you trust it, you
will find yourself energized with a feeling of
God's will. Now, if you don't pray, you're going
to have to pretty much do the same thing, except
you have to really ask the question out into space.
And you still have to wait patiently for the answer
to come.

I still remember when I realized that I needed to
divorce my wife. I was living with up and down
abuse, suspicion, and controlling stuff from her.
My home was not really emotionally safe for me.
But I have always liked to soak in the tub, and
often read. This refuge provided me some safety
in a turbulent house. And it was one evening,
reading and reflecting in the tub, that I realized
that my truth, what welled up within me, what
motivated and inspired me, was something that
she could never be expected to accept and allow to
flourish. It wasn't a thought, so much. It was a

feeling, deep down, that my purpose in life was greater than what I could accomplish with her.

For me, I call this my inner truth. It seems to come from outside my mind as a feeling. I can't explain why, but I have learned to trust this feeling. Ultimately, when we are put in situations that tear us emotionally, we have to find this feeling and trust it, because looking outside for the answer to "What should I do?" is guaranteed to give us somebody else's answer to our question. The only way to find our own answer is to ask the question and seek the answer.

This is the essence of finding yourself.

The Shadow of Death

I wrote the following when I was still living with my wife:

Well, I have a couple of hours alone at home. And I have company.

No, it's not a person. It's not a pet. It's not even invited.

It's the shadow of death. And everyone knows that if you follow a shadow along the ground in the direction of the sun, you'll find what's casting that shadow. And this one is cast by a petite little 100 lb. NEC wife.

Early in this saga, I read about the "old brain" or "reptile brain," a part of our brain rooted in the distant past, before humans were even human. It's a simple brain, which doesn't even really think. It just reacts to patterns. And like any good BP, it reacts in black and white. Things are unknown; or they're the source of life and goodness; or they're death approaching. Most of our primitive fear responses come from the old brain. So does falling in love, something that has influenced most of our lives.

When the old brain detects a pattern that matches death, it gives us an overpowering need to flee. And if we fight that urge, using our conscious thought, it still affects us. Our bodies react like a car with an automatic transmission, the brake pressed to the floor, and the gas halfway down: screaming, burning, begging for something to give. And we get high blood pressure, stress related pain, depression, and all that stuff that all of us have.

I live with the specter of death. Long, long ago, my old brain connected my wife with pain and death. And I live in fear all the time. Not that I can't function, but I'm in fear anyway. And it has made me sick, and is still making me sick.

And what really bothers me is being by myself at home. Because I cannot relax. I cannot lower the defenses against death—because death might walk in at any moment. And I hate it.

I escaped this specter once: when my wife was in inpatient rehab last summer, 30 miles away, with no car and no money. And my specter left. I liked it. I liked it a lot.

When I read Peck (*The Road Less Traveled*, p 165) much of this came together for me. It forced me to realize that it was NEVER going to get better and that my wife will always be the shadow of death to me. And I decided that I would succumb to that specter if I didn't free myself from it.

Yea, though I walk through the valley of the shadow of death, I shall fear no evil. But my friends, this can only last for so long. Eventually one must simply decide to find a safer place to walk.

Constancy of Perspective

Because our SOs go through such extreme cycles of emotion and behavior, and because these behaviors affect us so profoundly, it can be very, very difficult to keep a level perspective on what is happening. When you couple this with

- ➢ how awful the bad stuff is, and

- ➢ how positive the good stuff is

you end up alternating between a soup of dissociation and denial (the bad stuff isn't really that bad) when things are good, and being devastated and unable to think clearly during rages and acting out. Then it becomes impossible to resolve choices because you never have a calm, complete picture of what is happening to you.

Ultimately for me, I had to overcome this by building constancy of perspective - when it got bad I didn't go there, and when it got good I didn't go there. Read detaching here (p. 83), because this is really what it takes to do this. From this foundation I could then resolve what my choices needed to be. And this depended on knowing who and what I am.

So while you may realize that you are in tremendous distress in your relationship, you have two ways to go. You can either take precipitous action by leaving or separating, but you won't feel that you've made a measured decision because you can't make a measured decision. Or you can just hang in there, and try to build some constancy in your view of the relationship, so that you can make measured decisions without duress. Ultimately, regardless of what you decide, this second choice is where you'd like to go.

Detaching is hard. But it boils down to getting a factual understanding that there is a disease with strong effects operating, and feeling safe enough in yourself to allow those effects to roll out before you, on you, and around you without being swept up in them. It's hard, but it's really the only complete way to deal with your situation.

Depression and the Unconscious

I learned a lot from Peck (p. 165). You know, things happen in their own time, when they're ready, and there is a reason for things to happen. This book appeared in my house as if by divine intervention just when I needed it. And I needed it. (And maybe I needed it just to tell you about it because you needed it).

M. Scott Peck on Depression

Anyway, about depression: someone said there is a reason - and that's right. Peck's perspective fits so well. He says that we all have a private unconscious, and a common (to all man) unconscious, and that this is the final arbiter of what is right or wrong. When we are emotionally and spiritually healthy, we are in contact with our unconscious, and understand and follow its guidance.

But sometimes our conscious mind rejects the guidance of our unconscious. For example, when I was sticking out this relationship with my wife. I didn't have to meditate for more than about two nanoseconds to get my unconscious guidance on this issue. My unconscious wanted me to get away from her. Surprise! She was abusive, hurtful, and what's more, she hated my unconscious and the directions that it leads me. So my conscious mind, controlling my behavior, was in direct opposition to my unconscious guidance.

This leads to a very important result: depression. And Peck's writing finally got me clear that my tears are like a flashing red light - saying, "You're not listening to me!" And once I started listening, I realized that whenever I cried, it was because of this tension –this refusal to follow the guidance of my unconscious (p. 137). And usually there's a really specific message in what I feel at these moments.

Making Use Of This Understanding

Now, why would you care about this? Well, basically, you'll have to learn to listen to your unconscious (maybe even for longer than a nanosecond –or not) to discover what the tension is in your life. Maybe you already know what it is. But your depression might not go away by anti-depressing yourself. It might take more. It might take figuring out how you'll get your conscious mind on the same wavelength with your unconscious.

I'm finding it really helpful to have this framework to think about, because you can put a few other pieces of Peck's puzzle in to get more clarity. For example, he says that love (not romantic love, but the REAL stuff) consists of nurturing the spiritual growth of another person. That it takes effort and/or courage, and it reflects back and helps the giver grow, too.

I analyzed my marriage in light of that, and it came up short. So how was I going to grow, and how was I going get rid of my depression? I needed some change in my life, and having a clearer picture helped me. You see, you can't adjust your unconscious. So you have to work with your conscious. So I worked on finding ways to reorder my conscious thinking, to get it into better harmony with my unconscious truths, so that I could get rid of that depression, grow myself, and stop hurting all the time.

Parable of the Tree

A man lived in the Great Plains, many years ago. He had only one source of wood for all his needs: a beautiful large oak tree growing behind his cottage. Anyone passing by could see that this was truly a beautiful tree, and of course it was an oak tree so it must be strong. It would protect him from the prairie's storms and provide shade from the sun.

Chapter 4
Detaching and Finding Yourself

This man was very happy about his tree. It was really all he had ever wanted to meet his many needs. It was large enough to provide firewood from its fallen branches, its many limbs could be cut as he needed them for building furniture. The man was very happy.

One day the man decided to make a chair, so he took his saw and went out to his tree. He climbed onto one of the lower limbs and began to saw it off. As his saw bit into the wood, the man got a funny feeling. Something just didn't seem right. As he finished sawing the limb suddenly snapped as if it were brittle, shooting splinters into the man's eyes. He was surprised and hurt, but he managed to clear his eyes and slid down to where the limb had dropped to the ground.

He looked at the end where he had made his cut and to his amazement he saw not the solid, gleaming bands of a healthy oak, but a pithy, brittle mass riddled with holes. The limb would not serve for furniture - no way. And the man realized that something was amiss. He began having suspicions about his beautiful tree.

The next day the man tried again, for life presses on, and he really needed a chair. So he climbed again to another limb, and began cutting. And again, just as he was about to complete his task, the limb shattered and sprayed him with sharp splinters. This time he was prepared, and managed to turn his head, but the splinters were sharp and they hurt him nonetheless. Again he climbed down, and discovered the same pithy, brittle mass.

71

With this the man realized that his precious tree was not well. It was diseased. It was infested with an insect, the prairie oak flea, which was known to cripple trees, but not to kill them.

As the disease progressed, the man realized that he was not getting from his tree the things he counted on for his safety and comfort. The leaves became thin and scattered, and the tree could not provide the shade that he needed from the hot sun. When storms came, instead of the sheltering buffer he had hoped for, the tree would yield its weakened limbs to the winds and they crashed down on his cottage roof. Once a limb broke right through in the midst of a storm and the man spent a cold wet night waiting for daylight so he could close the hole.

But still, the man loved his tree. It was a beautiful tree. And it was an oak. It was HIS oak. "I love my tree," said the man. "I know it has a disease, but I love the tree nonetheless. I chose to build my home in its shelter and I am committed to staying with it."

One day a passing wagon stopped, and the man in the wagon asked, "Why do you stay under this sick tree? It's causing you so much pain, and there are things you need that it doesn't give you?"

"Oh, no," said the man. " I love my tree. It's the disease that I hate. The tree is still a beautiful tree, and it is my life."

"But look," said the man in the wagon. "Its wood is rotten. Its shade is useless. It harms you in

Chapter 4
Detaching and Finding Yourself

storms when it should shelter you. And you have no furniture because its wood is brittle and pithy."

"Oh, no," said the man. "You must learn to separate the disease from the tree. Otherwise you'll become embittered."

"Well," said the man in the wagon, "if the disease is separate, then where is the tree without the disease? I don't see a healthy tree standing next to a disease. All I see is a pithy, bug-eaten tree that can barely stand on its own. If your tree is such a good provider, why is that you have so little, and what you have is patched and leaking?"

The man thought for a while, and then said, "You know, maybe you are right. No matter how much I say I love that tree, it will never give me the things I need from it. I guess you're right. The TREE and the DISEASE are all the same thing. I don't have a tree and a disease. I have a DISEASED TREE. And the longer I hang out under this tree, the longer I'm going to live without the shade and the wind shelter and the furniture that I need, and the more likely I'm going to be conked on the head by a falling limb. Maybe I need to start looking for another tree that can give me what I need..."

The man thought about it, and a little later he decided to look around for another place to have his home. And the man found a spot, even better than the one he had been living in, with a healthy maple growing nearby.

He hated to think of building his home all over again, but he was, at heart, a courageous man, and he decided to try. In a few months he had a new home, shaded in the summer, shielded from the wind, safe during storms, and he was able to build beautiful furniture for his study. He lived there, mostly happily, writing to his many friends who also had problem trees.

His old tree continued to grow in its same spot, and continued dropping limbs during every storm, just as before.

The Metaphysics of Detaching

Just to show even famous philosophers don't always know what to say, I had a question on one of the lists about "how much detachment" sitting in my inbox for quite a long time, with no answer forthcoming. For me though, a little soak time usually cures that, *and* as a special added bonus, I am *actually* going to throw some genuine philosophy at you... Can you believe it? More importantly, are you *ready*?

Now before I wax too much here, I want to explain what I mean by *detaching*. This word seems to go in a lot of different directions in different people's minds. What I mean by *detaching* is distancing yourself emotionally from the actions, words, and feelings of another person. Now, as I have come to understand this from the Al-Anon literature, detaching is not a tactic you use in a given interaction. It is a fundamental change in emotional attitude toward another person. It is something that takes time and commitment, and hopefully stays with us *through* difficult interactions or situations. In the Al-Anon literature, detaching helps people to take better care of themselves while still living with a troubled person.

Detaching is a conscious choice to give less emphasis to the emotional impact another person has on us. Some people read "detaching" and think of "checking out" or "dissociating" during a rage. That's NOT what I mean by detaching. I mean granting less accessibility of your emotional state, long term, to the control or effects of another. Keep in mind, with BPs, they are often *trying* to make us feel badly. They manipulate our feelings to moderate their own pain. Other times they are out of control, unable to consider our well being, and flail at us in very hurtful ways. Detaching is accepting as an ongoing premise that "I won't care as much about this as I did before."

The Ultimate Obligation: Now the question here was "how much detaching?" It all comes down, in my mind, to what your ultimate obligation is. And I believe your ultimate obligation is to care for your own spirit.

Let me put this in religious words first, because this is probably a little more understandable. If we honestly assess our miniscule power in this world, and the vast scope of the world around us, we must conclude that there is a greater purpose in this world. Could God really love you so little that he would intend for you to slowly destroy yourself in a depriving and hurtful relationship? And if he did intend it, why did he give you the will and power to *choose*? Surely he intended for you to, above all, love yourself?

And now for the real philosophy. This all came together in kind of a blur. But yes, somewhere in my deep, dark memory, long before my wife messed with my head, is this repository of knowledge of (dare I say) ethics. And there lived long ago a real famous 18th century philosopher named Kant. Kant described his philosophy as metaphysical—dealing with the fundamental nature of reality or with things outside of objective experience. In particular I spent a good deal of time struggling with Kant's work, *A Groundwork of the Metaphysic of Morals*.

Kant's basic belief is that humans are unique in the world because we have been given a free will. And because we have free will, we have the power to *choose* to act in a moral or immoral way. And, through arguments that not even he can express simply, Kant concludes that the imperative for all moral beings is to act in harmony with what is right. Thus, the basis of a moral action must be valid as a moral principle for all moral beings. Another way to say this is, if the reason you choose your action is valid for all moral beings, then your action is a moral one. If the reason is not valid for all moral beings, then your action is not moral.

What does this mean for us nons? It means that, if a choice to stay in a demeaning and deprived relationship is morally right for one of us, that directly means that it is right for everyone. Let me say that differently. If you, as a non, choose to stay in a hurtful relationship, and at the same time you would **not**, as a rule, say that others in similar situations must also stay in their relationships, then your choice is not a moral choice. If you choose to care for yourself, by changing or leaving the relationship, and you can say, as a RULE, that everyone should similarly care for themselves, then this is a moral choice. Now I'm sure you can tell from the way I posed that, that I think caring for yourself is a moral choice.

So, go back now to the religious words: if God really loved you, would he intend for you to slowly destroy yourself in a depriving and hurtful relationship? Do you see how these tie together?

Well, that was certainly a lot words. And as Owl once said in the Pooh videos that I've watched with my children, "It takes quite a lot of words to say a thing like that." Now let's look at what this means in the context of whether to protect yourself or the relationship.

Two Issues: Self and Relationship

I was asked "Where is the line between detaching enough to care for yourself, and detaching so much that you put the relationship in jeopardy?"

This is the wrong way to think about it. There are really two continua. The first is the degree to which you choose to protect yourself. The second, which is separate, is how far you extend yourself to "foster" the relationship. They may interact, or they may not. But I think you need to think of those as separate.

Many people in long term relationships with troubled SOs have the priority very high on fostering the relationship, and very low on protecting themselves. And a lot of people in such situations end up in distress, so there is almost certainly something wrong with those priorities.

Now after all that, you know that I'm going to say that you need to place a high priority on caring for yourself. And if you don't go for the metaphysic of morals, I'll give you some more practical thoughts to support that caring for yourself is your most sacred obligation in this world, even more important that caring for your children, and distinctly more important than caring for your marriage.

Paramount: Caring for Yourself

Why? Because without a healthy and functioning you, you cannot fulfill your other obligations. You could look at the section on What About Me? (p. 115), and just to show that I sometimes actually practice what I preach, you can read a little about how not caring for your spiritual needs can lead to depression on Depression and Unconscious (p. 68), and also have a look at how my unconscious clobbered me for not taking enough care of myself, and fixed some of my values at the same time: On Changing Values (p. 117).

Now hopefully, if you read all that, you are convinced that the relationship *has* to come second. Now you're probably gasping. But think about it. If your relationship was healthy, and was with a healthy spouse, would this be a problem in ANY way? Not a chance. The fact that your own well-being is in direct conflict with fostering the relationship is a big, *BIG* signal that something is really wrong.

Deciding What *You* Need

The way I'd like you to look at this is to focus on *you*. What do you need to be healthy? I'll bet if you seriously reflect on this, you'll be close to tears, which is a subconscious signal that what you're thinking of is something that would be healing for you. You can look at Tears and Healing (p. 137) for a lot more on this. And then you need to decide whether you are getting that, or whether there is any likelihood that you'll get it in the reasonable future in your current relationship.

If the answer is no, then you need to take steps to make it possible to get what you need. I really don't think there is any real choice. First of all, Kant said so, and besides, if you gut it out, you will continue to starve yourself spiritually. Bad things happen when you do this, including depression and, God forbid, falling in love with someone else (check the section On Changing Values (p. 117) for my sad story on this). You should also plug in the thoughts about real love and loving relationships from Love vs. In-Love (p. 89).

Now, if you are getting what you need, or there is good chance you will, you can focus your energy on the relationship. But what if you are not?

Protecting Yourself by Detaching

If the relationship is really harming you, and you cannot reasonably foresee a change that will remedy that, you have to start protecting yourself. Detaching is a way of distancing yourself emotionally from the actions, words, and feelings of another person. Al-Anon is great at teaching this. Basically, you start to redefine what makes you ok and to focus on that. It is like emotionally circling the wagons. You push your spouse's actions and pain outside of your circle. You focus on you and what you need and what you need to feel. A simple example is staying awake worrying when your spouse stays out late. You stop that. You go to bed and go to sleep. You focus on you and what you need. You leave your spouse's problems with your spouse. You decide to be OK no matter *what* is happening out there.

Now, you know this is going to cause big problems with a BP or an NEC or any seriously troubled spouse – because it is equivalent to abandoning them. And their behavior is likely to change. When I wrote to one list member whose spouse was consistently escalating the emotional violence, I was pretty pessimistic. I think his situation might very well be unstable (speaking as an engineering-type guy). The more he detaches, the more forceful her violence will be, prompting him to detach more, prompting more violence. In chemical plants these unstable type situations end up in devastating explosions (so they hire smart guys like me to make sure they don't happen) . But we're not talking about molecules here; we're talking about a disordered spouse who is in great emotional pain. It is a sad reality of most of these relationships.

If your spouse is less sick, functioning better, has good psychological support, or other helpful factors are present, then you may find that the relationship improves. Your own care for yourself may provoke a realization that the bar has been raised for membership in the relationship, and your spouse may get more serious about changing. But the reality is that the relationship is not under your control. Only you are under your control, and the best thing you can do is to take care of you.

Detaching Disconnects the Relationship

Unfortunately, I find the Al-Anon literature is a little optimistic. Because I really do not believe you can maintain an intimate relationship with someone that you are detaching from. The problem is that intimacy requires trust so that vulnerabilities can be shared. Well, let's face it, this isn't happening to begin with in relationships of those who are asking these questions. But if you add detaching, you surely lose the trust and sharing of vulnerabilities, and this by itself makes the relationship not an intimate one. And so detaching has to go one of two ways: it either serves as a catalyst - raising the bar, as I said earlier - to get a spouse to seek change, or it will be the first step in ending the relationship and making room in your life for a relationship that *can* be intimate.

Now, I tried to consider whether there are SOME situations in which it might be practically necessary to preserve the relationship even though it is really hurting the non. And, frankly, I cannot think of any real reason to continue to harm yourself for a relationship that is ***doing*** that harming. If you cannot achieve some safety by detaching, then you have to seriously look at getting out, at least long enough to bring some change.

Some things take time, like finding a job, etc. That is part of the process. But I honestly can think of no practical reasons that justify just staying and allowing more and more deprivation and harm to yourself without taking steps to protect and sustain yourself.

Well, it all comes down to a few sentences, even after all that analysis. Your obligation is to care for yourself. When you do this, a partially well partner may well respond by rising to the challenge and finding ways to heal; or it will be the first step toward ending the relationship. There you go: your future in two sentences.

So, you're not ready to accept all this? Or you don't like Kant??!!! Well, I never! No, really, this is OK. I don't expect you to simply accept all this. It's not that easy. It takes time and effort to come to terms with all this. Keep reading, keep thinking, keep exploring deep down for what is really right. You might find you do like green eggs and Kant.

Detaching and Dimensions of Relationships

Well, talking about detaching seems to generate questions about whether it is possible to detach from someone while staying in the relationship. I thought about this, and I think this may be confusing just from lack of precise definition. I'll try to split this hair a little finer.

My belief is that detaching puts emotional distance between two people. When one person detaches because of significant harm being done by their partner, I believe this emotional distancing is also significant.

Detaching Interferes with Intimacy

One thing affected by detaching is intimacy. By that I mean trust, sharing of burdens, sharing of vulnerabilities, and mutual caring support. Let's call these the characteristics of an intimate relationship.

There are many other dimensions of relationships. Living together is a very important one. Parenting children together is another big one. Sharing financial burdens is another. You can think of many more, I'm sure.

So one way to split this hair of detachment is by looking at the different effects it has on *intimate* relationships vs. the effects on other types of relationships. I believe that significant detaching will significantly impair the intimate relationship.

However, it is quite possible to detach and still maintain other types of relationship, like living together, etc.

The important point to see here is that if you are married or have an exclusive non-married relationship, if you detach from your partner, you are (to some degree) blocking your sole source of that intimate trust, sharing of burdens, etc. You are essentially going on an *emotional fast* with respect to those things - things that in our culture ONLY come through that exclusive relationship. And while this might be something that helps correct problems or works out best in the long run, it is a state of deprivation that is harmful to you.

Other Relationship Dimensions Can Continue

Maintaining the other relationships: living together, co-parenting, etc, may help deal with other demands in life. These are reasonable concerns. But emotional deprivation is an insidious current that undermines our ability to be healthy and function well. So it must be seriously considered even when other life demands point toward maintaining the other relationship dimensions. Having a home and two parents and paying the bills is not much good if you become too distressed to do what you need to do in life. If you're not convinced, go read On Changing Values (p. 117).

So again, my suggestion is to ask whether you are getting what you need to stay healthy and function well. If the answer is no, it's probably time to consider what you can change to get those things.

Detaching and the Disease/Person Paradox

Talking about detaching always raises a common idea: detaching from the *behavior* and not the person. I think Al-Anon more often uses the words *disease* and person. I disbelieve this can be done, but maybe it is matter of definitions.

I'll refer back to the way I divided the relationship dimensions around detaching in Detaching and Relationship Dimensions (p. 83). I believe that, when you are talking about a chosen relationship—marriage as the primary example— the intimate aspect of the relationship is really of *primary* importance. The marriage simply can't function without intimacy. So from the perspective of having a functioning marriage, I think that significantly detaching makes the marriage not a functioning marriage. This is what I think of when I think of detaching from the disease and not the person.

From this perspective, detaching from the disease *does* detach from the person-spouse. In other words, for a spouse, when you detach from a significant harmful behavior, you *DO* detach from that person as your spouse.

It is still possible to detach and maintain those other aspects of relationship: living together, co-parenting, sharing finances, etc. So, to make the

Al-Anon wording make sense for me, detaching from the disease and not the person means detaching emotionally but keeping the living together, co-parenting, etc.

After long reflection, I finally rejected the idea that a fundamental disease like a personality disorder could be treated separately from the person. I believe they are one and the same. I've written twice about this: Onions and Scrambled Eggs (p. 44), and Parable of the Tree (p. 70).

Al-Anon on Letting Go

At a time when things felt so terribly beyond my control, Al-Anon books helped me acknowledge my feelings and come to better acceptance of what was happening. One passage in particular helped me when my wife was in crisis. For whatever reason, Al-Anon feels their books should not be quoted at all except within their own groups. I can only wonder how a public service organization arrives at such a position, especially one not supported by U.S. copyright law.

Notwithstanding, the basic idea taught is this: It sounds like a simple thing to let go and let God. Yet when a spouse or loved one is in crisis, we want to hang on at all costs. It seems like doing whatever we can to maintain some control can prevent bad things from happening. We fear that if we give up control, anything could happen.

But when we try to maintain control, what we really do is to lock ourselves into a horrible situation. And, in reality, all our efforts aren't working to stop bad things from happening. The control we think we are maintaining is really an illusion.

And so, in backhanded way, we are right. If we give up control, anything could happen, even something much, much better than we imagined. When we stop trying to control things, we open the door to change.

When we stop controlling, the natural consequences of actions start to be felt. Whether our partner is drinking uncontrollably, or raging, or despondent, or whatever, releasing control often means that the consequences of their actions start to come home to them. For example, an abusive partner might end up in jail if we call the police, or an addicted partner might be disciplined for missing work if we don't cover for them. We might think these are terrible things we're allowing to happen, but in reality, people respond to the consequences of their actions. If these consequences seem awful to us, they also seem awful to them. And awful consequences can be a strong motivator to change.

By releasing control and having faith that in time things will work out, we open the door to life changes that can make our lives much, much better. To do this takes faith – faith that we have the power to build a better life; faith that even when things seem terribly hard, they will get better.

Looking back at my situation at its worst, I know now that the best thing to do situation was not what I thought it was. I wanted to hold on at all costs to the "situation," and I've written about how I felt obligated to my wife and my children and the grocery store clerk (p. 113). I thought above all I needed to preserve a nuclear family and blah blah blah...

Ultimately, I had to let go and let things find their own course. For me, that led to separation, and a lot of time and effort to ensure our children were well cared for. I've written about how this responsible care for them enabled them to sail through separation without emotional trauma, or even an apparent hiccup. My then-wife has improved significantly after three years on her own. And, yes, I am better off now too.

Faith allows amazing things to happen.

Chapter 5
Dealing with "Love"

Love vs. In-Love

Well, everybody is always talking about love. And with so many people saying so many things about it, I guess it makes sense to understand what this simple, four-letter word means. So let's borrow from Harville Hendrix (p. 163) and M. Scott Peck (p. 165) yet again. Right off the top let's break this into two very big and very different pieces. Let's think of love, loving, and the act of love on the one hand, and falling in love, being in love, and romantic love on the other hand. And to really talk about these things and understand, you need to know which one you've got and which one you don't.

Briefly, *falling in love* is an unconsciously motivated insane state in which we attempt to meet our own needs, to make up for not caring enough for ourselves, by completing ourselves in sexual union with and emotional dependence on another person. *Loving* is a chosen, purposeful effort, often done in the face of fear, to nurture our own spiritual growth or the growth of another.

Wow. Are you still with me? I know this seems pretty radical, but there is a lot here you can use to get in control of your life. Trust me.

Falling In Love: Old black and white movies; *Beauty and the Beast*; happily ever after. Man, we all want to fall in love. It's the way the universe tells us who we belong with forever and ever. And nothing could be better. Except...

Falling in love is mental illness in disguise. Mental illness?!! Yes, that's what I said. Falling in love is mental illness in disguise. Here's a short catalog of what's wrong with falling in love:

- First, we're overcome with excitement, fulfillment, and euphoria. Hello? From being close to someone who we might not even know? Doesn't sound very healthy to me.

- Second, we lose all perspective about the person we're in love with. We idealize the person. They become the most beautiful/handsome, most loving, caring, kindest... Really?

- Third, being in love doesn't last. The fairy tales say it will. And sometimes we might know a couple that is still "in love" after 40 years. But it's not so. Eventually reality sinks in and the glow is lost. Being in love is just a transient state of altered consciousness. That 40 year couple isn't in love, they've transitioned to loving, which is totally different.

- Fourth, we lose ourselves. Without our understanding it, our whole ego tries to merge with our love. We become incomplete without them. We need that person to be whole. Nice romantic concept. But not very healthy. Have you ever been in love with someone who didn't love you back? I have. And it isn't very healthy. Trust me.

- Fifth, we can't control it. We don't choose to fall in love, and we don't choose who we fall in love with. Hendrix has a great theory, called imago theory, that explains who we'll fall in love with. But it isn't up to us.

- Sixth, falling in love is always sexual. It just won't happen outside of that, because it is driven by our sexual drives.

So, when you're in love:

- You get there without choice;

- You didn't get to choose who you're in love with;

- The one you're in love with has to be from the limited set of people you can be sexually attracted to;

- You can't think straight, because everything is idealized;

- You can't feel straight, because you're lost in euphoria (or dysphoria if she doesn't love you back); and

- You can't be whole by yourself.

As nice as euphoria is, you can do a lot of damage to yourself when you're lost in this fog. There's a little more on this feeling of euphoria in Magical Stuff (p. 54).

The Incomplete Self: Why do we go there? We go there because, by ourselves, we are incomplete. When we are incomplete, we are unhappy. Now, you can read Hendrix (p. 163) to get a lot more detail about this. He says we deny parts of ourselves, and we lose parts of ourselves.

- We deny parts because family and society disapprove. I might be a big hulking guy and love floral wallpaper. Not for long, I guess. It would be too painful. Better to just deny that part of me and go with plain off-white.

- We lose parts of ourselves because we fail to recognize them and don't nurture them. For example, I might have been an athlete in high school, but in my years studying quantum mechanics and later working hard at the laboratory bench trying to count all those quanta, I could lose the physical aspect of myself.

Chapter 5
Dealing with "Love"

These denied and incomplete parts are more than just empty spaces. They are unmet needs. As people, we are not complete without them. They are deficiencies in our spirit. We cannot fulfill ourselves without them. They are aspects of ourselves in which we need to grow. And neglecting these aspects of ourselves makes us sick, too. It causes malaise and depression. Have a look at Depression and the Unconscious (p. 68).

To grow, we are going to need to expend some effort. We are going to need to take some risk. We are going to need nurturing. In other words, we are going to need some spiritual growth to overcome these deficiencies.

Which brings us to love.

Love: Peck (p. 165) says it better than I can, but, to paraphrase, love is work or courage expended to nurture the spiritual growth of myself or another. It is a choice. And it is hard. No idealism here. No euphoria. No loss of ourselves. And no agony if it isn't returned.

What is spiritual growth? It is the growth of ourselves as human beings - as complete human beings. Hendrix talks about four aspects: physical, sexual, thinking, and feeling. To be complete, to be spiritually fulfilled, we need to develop all four of these parts of ourselves.

Now, let's say you grew up in a family situation where you were told that you were dumb and shouldn't expect to succeed at anything "hard."

You might have made choices that steered you away from developing your thinking capabilities. As an adult, you're probably not going to suddenly start studying quantum mechanics or relativistic physics. To develop this part of you, you will probably need some help. You will need the effort and persistence of someone who can assist or guide you in developing your thinking skills. This effort is love, and assists you in your spiritual development.

The same might be true of your sexuality. If you were influenced to avoid those aspects of your emotions and ignored the physical signals from your body, you are probably going to need some help to develop a healthy sexuality. That might come from a counselor, a doctor, or a caring intimate partner. But it is going to take some effort, and that effort is going to have to be focused on you and helping you grow.

One From Column A, One From Column B:
Now, let's start lacing these two together. Did you notice that both falling in love and love are ways to complete yourself - to fill in the missing pieces?

Now, here you are, incomplete, as we all are. There is a driving force to change that - that's why we fall in love! Now, you have a choice. You can try to fill in those holes by falling in love, or you can try to fill them in through love. Which are you going to chose? Well, love is work. That's not too enticing. Falling in love feels good. Yeah, that's for me!

Chapter 5
Dealing with "Love"

The problem is that falling in love has so many problems. Go back up and look at that list again. Just limiting the people could help you grow to those who could be sexually attractive is a huge limitation. Think of all the potential that's eliminated! And the other problems are big, too. Taken together, they almost guarantee that falling in love won't provide the growth that you need. It's a deception, a dirty trick of nature.

In fact, both Peck and Hendrix argue that falling in love is a Darwinian development designed to fool us into starting families, and might by luck even set us up to get real love. But by itself, falling in love is not going to fill in those holes. Only the growth made possible by love is going to do that. And in case I wasn't clear, falling in love is so dysfunctional that no real love will happen in that state of mind.

No Alternative to Love: So the reality is that, sooner or later, you are going to have to get some **real** love if you're going to be complete. That means you're going to be unhappy until you get it. And you may fall in love again and again, each time being swept up in the euphoria and distorted thinking, believing *this time* all your needs will be filled, and still not get there. If we're lucky, a falling-in-love relationship will evolve into a loving relationship, and that will help us grow. But if you're reading this, it probably didn't happen for you.

The great thing about real love is that it can come from anyone: from an 89 year old chemistry professor; a therapist we pay to help us; some loud mouth on the Internet; the author of an inspirational book. Real love is about *people*, not about sex. Real love is healthy and sustaining, so you can get it where you want, when you want, with whom you want. And you can keep your head and your emotions with you. It is truly a healthy interaction.

We all need energy and courage invested in us to help us grow. We need someone - and it could be someone else or we can do it ourselves - to care enough to work to help us overcome our fears, learn the things we didn't know, unlearn the wrong things we've learned (that's what I'm doing here, I hope), and step onto new ground. It takes time. And it *is* work. And it's not very likely to come from falling in love.

But it is the only way to become truly happy. And the need to complete this task will never go away. Not as long as we live. It is, in truth, *the* challenge of being human.

What to Grow? Great, you're thinking, all I have do is fix up these hidden and denied parts of myself --- wait a minute?! How the heck do I know what these parts are?

This is a hard question. Obviously once you break through the denial enough to see the denied parts, they won't be denied anymore. The hidden parts you probably know, if you have the courage to look. But how?

Chapter 5
Dealing with "Love"

Well, I think there may be lots of ways to get at this, but the one that I think has been most definitive for me is the pointer of tears. I talk more about this in the section on Tears and Healing (p. 137). But for now let me just say that, in general, things that give you a teary, hurt feeling are things that are *about* your hidden and denied aspects. I'll give you a couple of examples.

Example 1: Performing - I used to sit in my daughters' ballet recitals with tears in my eyes. There was no great mystery about it. I *knew* that I was wishing that I could perform for an audience. I was really jealous of the opportunity my children had. This was an undeveloped aspect of my spirit, making its need felt through tears. Well, one of the activities I've found for myself is a performing sport. It's done before an audience, and people like to watch. I didn't know when I took it up that I was fulfilling a part of myself that had been neglected. But I was, and I know now that this is one aspect that continues to draw me. And I feel very different watching others perform now. I don't feel jealous or sad; I *relate* to what they're doing.

Example 2: Help Me! - I used to find myself welling up, almost sobbing, when an ambulance would pass with lights and siren. I would think about how ambulance crews devote themselves selflessly to helping others in desperate need. This had happened for a long time, but I never understood it. Now I do understand.

I was in an unhealthy relationship for a long time. My wife controlled me and dominated my spirit. Even as I was growing and building some new aspects of myself, she resorted to more desperate and violent verbal attacks to beat me down. So what does that have to do with an ambulance? I had isolated myself from people and from the nurturing that was around me in the world. And I *needed* the help and nurture of those people. My spirit was calling out to me, "Help me!" And I wasn't listening.

Step by Step - I know these are small things, and they're about me, not about you. But I bet you have a little store of situations, places, people, movie scenes, or whatever, that give you similar feelings. These things are pointing to the areas you need to develop: aspects of yourself about which you need to find people willing to give to you, and help you grow.

Those people are out there. They're teaching art classes, on Internet support lists, at the end of the telephone line to that relative you've stopped talking to, and a thousand other places. We each have to reach out to find them.

Why Am I In Love?

You know, this question is *so* important - because it cuts to the heart of nearly all the issues that plague us in these relationships.

You are in love because you haven't fulfilled yourself, and your unconscious mind is trying to find someone else to make that happen. And it

very often doesn't work. In fact, it often makes
things worse.

Think about what you want from a relationship
that is based on being in love: I'll call it an in-love
relationship. By in-love I mean falling into
romantic love, head-over-heels, can't live without
her kind of stuff. What do you want? Sex and
nurturing. Let's think a minute about nurturing.
What kind of things do we do in these intimate, in-
love relationships that we don't do in our other
relationships? We allow ourselves to be
emotionally dependent on our partner. We drop
our strong, silent front, stop pretending we are
everything, and lean on our partner.

In a word, we act like children. We ask our partner
to play a parenting role with us. We push off
responsibility for at least part of our well being,
and expect our partner to make things right. We
accept ourselves as incomplete and *we seek to feel
complete through another person*.

The best explanation I have found for this is by
Hendrix (p. 100). Hendrix believes we have two
ways we force ourselves to be incomplete. The
first is *denying* parts of ourselves, and the second
is *hiding* parts of ourselves. Both are aspects of
our being, our spirit, that we refuse to express, the
first because we cannot accept that we have those
traits, and the second because we fear others'
reactions to those traits.

So again, why are you in love? To complete
yourself by using another person to provide the

denied and hidden aspects of yourself. Don't want to be in love? Find your whole self. Love your whole self. I can't say I've achieved this, but I believe it is the path to emotional and spiritual health, and that risk of falling in-love goes down as we move down that path.

Falling in love is an unconscious mechanism that tries to compensate our own failure to fully realize our full self. Accept yourself, know yourself, love yourself. By this you can free yourself from the trap of falling in-love yet again.

Why Do I Long for <u>Her</u>? - Imago Theory

I hear this question a lot, and since I worked hard to get a plausible explanation of this for myself, I want to offer this short discourse on **Imago Relationship Theory**, attributable to Hendrix.

Imago - Each of us forms an Image (called an imago – pronunciation: i mah go) based on the characteristics of our primary caregivers as young children. This subconscious image includes the shortcomings in those people, including how we were hurt or neglected. It determines who we will fall in love with. When we meet an imago match, we quickly feel like we've always known him, we can't remember being without him. We feel that we aren't complete without him, that we must have him. Our subconscious is overjoyed at finding the person who once had cared for us, and will now resume and make everything right.

Chapter 5
Dealing with "Love"

Romantic love overwhelms us and makes us behave in unselfish ways, and see only the good in the person. Invariably this peters out (usually soon after engagement or marriage) and the person hurts us in the same way as our childhood caregivers (this is why they match our image), and we are ill prepared to deal with this. The relationship falters, and if both partners cannot grow to overcome the weaknesses that they have, the relationship will fail. By this time, our subconscious has caught on that this person isn't going to make everything right, and we are ready to go find another imago match. This is commonly called falling out of love.

The bad news is that these feelings of necessity are very strong early in the relationship. The good news: there are *lots* of imago matches in the world, and you can find others if you work at it. More bad news: since you failed in your first relationship, and didn't overcome your weaknesses, you'll do it all over again.

If you're not used to thinking about how your mind and feelings work together, this might sound like psycho-babble. But it is a very powerful model that fits with real life experience. It really helped me to move on when my subconscious went out and found a near-clone of my BPW and flattened me into love with her. So theories like this can help you see what's happening in a different way, makes better choices about how you react, and move on to feeling better.

Hendrix has at least two books: *Getting the Love You Want* (for couples) and *Keeping the Love You Find* (for singles) (p. 163). They're wordy but well worth the time and effort if you are struggling to understand why you are so in love with someone, or how to get out of love with someone who is bad for you.

I'm In Love - How Do I Change It?

OK, you're in love. And you're reading a book about healing from abusive relationships, so it's a pretty good guess that you're not here to celebrate. You are probably hurting *big time*.

Let's try to get at what is happening. Again, the models I found helpful are Peck's and Hendrix's. Both agree that "falling in love" is essentially an insane state. Since intimate relationships are scary, and since they take a lot of work to get started, we might never find our way into them without help. So nature assists by genetically programming us to fall in love as a way to hook us into a permanent relationship.

The problem is that insanity is insane. Being in love compromises our ability to control our own lives. Our ego boundaries are compromised, and we don't feel whole in and of ourselves. And our reasoning about our lover is short circuited with blatant idealizations.

To deal with the "what do I do while I'm in love?" side, you need to look a little deeper. Remember that falling in love is a vehicle to get our emotional needs met. It's a means to fill in the incomplete parts of ourselves. So if you want to get unstuck from being in love with your BP, then you are going to have to find a way to meet your needs without him or her. Or better yet, through yourself.

Chances are, no matter what you do, the intense emotions will not pass quickly. However, there are some things you can do that will expedite the process.

First of all, you can start working on developing those unrealized parts of yourself. If you can develop the puzzle piece and put it into place, your unconscious mind won't need to go out fishing for it in your lover. You'll become happier and more complete in and of yourself, and you'll reduce the in-love drive to meet the need through another.

Second, you can take advantage of the mechanism your unconscious used to get you in love in the first place. Your unconscious was essentially shopping for someone to fall in love with. Remember the image - the pattern for who you will fall in love with? That's the shopping list. Well, your unconscious has bought model A. And that's who you're in love with.

But Hendrix teaches us that the imago is a vague pattern, having blurred, general features. There are thousands of people who match our patterns. So if we can do some conscious shopping, our unconscious is going to be coming along on those trips. And it's very possible, especially if we're not seeing the object of our in-love feelings any more, that our unconscious might decide that model B looks pretty good, too.

So, while it may feel totally empty and false to you, by exposing yourself to others, you enable your unconscious mechanisms to work - the same mechanisms that got you in love with the person you're in love with now. That mechanism might just up and change your feelings around to point toward somebody else. And if you're reading this, that somebody, chances are, couldn't be much worse than what you've got, and they might be a darned sight better.

But you have to be around other people for that to work. So getting around other people is critical to moving on. Your unconscious isn't too swift, and especially if it's already hooked on someone, it might take a lot of exposure to capture its attention. But being around people is good for us anyway, so this remedy can't possibly hurt, even if it's not entirely successful.

Now, I have a third idea. Falling in love drives us toward potential sexual partners. Our sexual drive is an essential piece of what makes this go. So falling in love is, in part, a way to get sex. Well, if you don't like the way you're being driven to get sex by your unconscious, you might try getting some with your conscious. Again, by proactively meeting your own needs, you reduce the drive toward falling you into love that your unconscious has. And this fits in just great with the last remedy of being around people. If you're gonna be around people, you might as well enjoy it.

Chapter 5
Dealing with "Love"

It won't be fast, and not likely easy, either. But working on your undeveloped self, exposing yourself to many others, and meeting your sexual needs by chosen relationships can all help to extricate you from the clutches of your unconscious who has fallen you into love with someone who is bad for you.

Codependence and Love

I was just listening to Celine Dion's *Because You Loved Me*. If you don't know it, it can be summed up in one line: "I'm everything I am because you loved me."

When I was in the depths of pain, this song really wrenched at me. I *so* much wanted to make her everything she is (unspecified her, at this point).

Later, as I learned more, I came to associate this feeling with codependence. That is, I thought it meant that I would only feel ok if there was someone out there who needed me for her to be ok. Well, one more problem to fix. After that, I made a real conscious effort to react to this song differently - by being aware that it was generating some feelings I thought were unhealthy and basically turning it off, at least mentally.

As you might have picked up, I'm a soft core Jungian, and I believe in a spirit within each of us that empowers us, provides our life energy, tries to guide us to be healthy, but struggles to communicate with our consciousness. The channel to my spirit that I discovered first was the channel of tears. When we experience something, usually something good, and we well up, this is a message from the spirit. There is something important, probably an unmet need, relating to that experience. You can read about this in the section Tears and Healing (p. 137).

I've since found another, much more controllable path to my spirit. It is through meditation. That is, in a safe and quite place, basically emptying my mind of the whirlwind of thoughts, putting a simple image in my awareness, and just being open to what is happening. If the image has to do with something important, my spirit responds with emotion. It may be a sustaining feeling, it may be tears, or it may be a sickening feeling in my stomach. This is the approach I used when I was in anguish about what to do with my marriage when my wife was slowly and methodically tearing me apart.

Another way of painting images in a meditative way is with music. In fact music connects with our spirit even without meditating, but by adding the quiet, safe space, I think I can get a much clearer picture of what my spirit is saying. And music was the channel by which I gained some better insight into what I thought was a codependent tendency in myself. Indeed, it was a LeAnn Rimes song, *I Believe in You,* that did this trick for me. This song's message is about feelings toward someone that loves you: "your mercy has no end, you're more than just a friend, it amazes me that you feel the way you do. I believe in you." (I can't even write these words without welling up, which gets back to the role that tears play.)

Chapter 5
Dealing with "Love"

This song helped me sort some of this out. The spiritual issue here is NOT that I'm a codependent that needs someone to need me to be ok. The issue here is one of *being appreciated* for loving someone. I never felt that my wife really received or appreciated the love I gave her. No matter what I did, it usually not enough. Or when it was, the way she expressed her acceptance and appreciation was very mechanical and insincere.

I don't know about you, but I really am a very loving person. And I loved my wife - and I mean in Peck's sense of caring and working for her. For so many years, my love was unacknowledged - unaccepted at a level that my spirit, the true judge of right and wrong, could recognize. And when my spirit senses the imagery in these songs, of love received, accepted, appreciated, and that appreciation is expressed beautifully, it sends me a really clear message. I need that. I need someone that can accept my love and show me so.

So, something that looked on the surface like a maladjustment in what I needed from an intimate relationship turned out underneath to be a fundamental message of growth for me. I do need it, and it's a healthy thing I need.

I'm still looking for that special person. I'm sure she's here somewhere. Has anybody seen her around?

Tears and Healing

Chapter 6
Obligation – The Hook

Obligation is a critical factor in non-BP relationships. Many of us get into our relationships because we fall in love, or to fill in missing or denied parts of our whole self. But we end up staying in them because of *obligation*.

Obligation, quite simply, is the thought that we *must* do something because of a requirement or expectation of someone or something that is *outside* our own needs and wants. And often, our concepts of obligation run completely contrary to our needs. We know we want something else; we know we need something else; but we persist in what we're doing because we believe that we *must*. Thus, obligation is what hooks us in and locks us down in hurtful relationships.

My thoughts on these issues have been shaped by Peck's (p. 165) writing and by Al-Anon books (p. 163). But just as important is the personal insight I've gained from working through my own obligation issues, and helping others on my support lists (p. 32) work through theirs.

Staying to be "Faithful"

We of course feel a sense of obligation to our spouses, and to those with whom we have long-term intimate relationships without marriage. Our wedding vows promise to love until death do we part. Our culture encourages us to think of marriage as something that can be lifelong; that should be lifelong.

There are two problems with this fairy tale approach to marriage, and both of them work to lock us in even when the marriage is literally tearing us apart:

The first problem with these ideas is that they don't take into account that *marriage must be a two-way process*. The idea that each partner is committed to love and care for the other no matter what is just not realistic. Some mountains are just too high to climb. We are human beings, and we have a right to depend on some commitment to us, just as our partners have that right.

We cannot force ourselves to continue on in a relationship in which we suffer trying to meet our partners seemingly endless needs, yet our partners are unable or unwilling to help us meet ours. A relationship cannot work if it becomes predominantly a one-way process.

The second problem this causes is that we fail to realize that our spouses must be first and foremost responsible for themselves. We allow ourselves to be trapped in the idea that we must be responsible for what our spouses do and what might happen to them. The truth is that **we can *never* be responsible for another adult**, nor should we try to be.

Our spouses must own their problems. They must bear the consequences of their own choices. They must suffer the pain of their own illnesses. This is not our burden to bear. I stayed with my wife through a time where I knew full well that I hated the relationship, needed more for myself, and saw no hope. Yet I thought she would die if I left her, and that her death would be my responsibility.

Ultimately, she almost did die even though I stayed with her. But it was never my burden to keep her alive. It was not my job to enable her to live with her pain and her illness even while she avoided trying to heal. I sickened myself and her by taking that on.

We must allow our spouses to own their own lives, their own behaviors, and the consequences of those.

Staying "For the Kids"

Feelings of parental obligation seem to me to be the strongest force that keeps people in hurtful relationships.

We tend to believe that to be a good parent, we must provide our children with an intact family above all else. To this end, we tolerate abuse, isolation, and even allow our relationship with the children - the same children we seek to protect and nurture - to be limited and damaged.

Here again, there are problems with this "must":

Options - We assume that an intact family is always better. We don't think about what it means to that family when one parent is ill and out of control. We don't consider how a healthy parent's interaction with the children is dominated, restricted, and limited by the dysfunction in the home. And we don't consider what the potential is for the children to have relationships in a different family structure - one where one healthy parent is truly free to have a full, healthy relationship with the children.

Modeling - We don't consider the impact on the children of the modeling we give in an unhealthy family. Children learn to do what they live with. In a dysfunctional home, children learn dysfunction. It's not realistic to think that a family with one parent who becomes dysphoric, acts out, rages, and puts their emotions before all others – even if it is only some of the time - can model for children a healthy relationship. We ignore the damage that the dysfunctional modeling does, and we ignore the potential to model a healthy relationship for them with a healthy partner.

Safety - We become so used to abuse, so accustomed to using our adult skills to cope with abuse and dysphoria, that we don't realize the home may not be emotionally safe for the children. Really, in our obligations as a parent, the safety of the children must be among the first – certainly more urgent and important than providing an intact family model. Yet our own psychological defenses – denial and even dissociation – prevent us from understanding how potentially unsafe the home may be.

Nons are usually devoted to their children. But understanding the whole picture, with all the trade-offs in providing what our children need, is essential if we are to free ourselves from blind obligation to keep them in an intact but dysfunctional family.

What Will "They" Think?

There is yet another "must" that works on many of us. Certainly it was a major force for me. This is the feeling that "they" will think badly of us. "They" are parents, neighbors, friends, relatives, coworkers, doctors, grocery store cashiers, and on, and on, and on.

This kind of obligation is about our sense of ourselves. Really, most of us rarely interact in ways that touch on our family situation except in very limited circles. Yet this feeling of "everyone" watching us – judging us – can be very strong. And since "they" are really not watching that much at all, it really is us who are watching ourselves.

Ultimately, it boils down to a preconception we carry around with us. Probably in large part it comes from the positive strokes we have received over the years. We have been appreciated for being a good father, a good mother, for having "made a success" of our lives, and so on. We accept that to be "good" we have to go on in this mode, and if we don't, we'll be condemned by others. And we feel this is important.

For some of us, this can be a challenge, because to overcome this we must come to know ourselves in a different way. The thought that "I am a good father because I have a job and a home and an intact nuclear family" needs to be set aside. It needs to be replaced with thoughts that are centered in more basic ideas. "I am a good father because I care about my children. I have the courage to truthfully assess the goodness of their lives. I am willing to do what is needed to make them most complete." And, as I'll talk about in the next section, "I am a good man because I love and care for myself."

So ultimately, we must seek out the basic ideas that motivate our lives. These are our morals, our deep values. They have to be deep enough to transcend situations, so we can use them to judge situations. Then, when we decide to make changes that run contrary to what we think "they" want, we can feel secure that we have acted in accordance with our deep values; that indeed, although "they" may not feel comfortable with what we have chosen, we know that we have done the right thing.

What Happened to Me?

The one person, and the one obligation, that is neglected most by nons is the obligation to one's self.

We are taught in life to persist. We are taught to finish the job, not to give up. We are taught, in short, to use our will to push ourselves to do the "right" things. And this is a big, big problem for many of us.

Feelings Over Thoughts: The problem with acting in accordance with our will is that it puts our *thoughts* in charge to override our *feelings*. The idea is that we know with our thoughts what is right, and our feelings are selfish, weak, greedy, lustful, and otherwise wrong. So our feelings make us want to do things, but our correct and right-minded thoughts tell us what is really right, and will provides the force that makes the thought prevail over the feeling.

And the thing that is so terribly wrong in this model is that our thoughts are never more right than our feelings. *Could it be so?*

Peck (p. 165) speaks to this very nicely, and the section on Depression and the Unconscious (p. 68) summarizes his view. When we use will to enforce our thoughts, we sicken ourselves - because we are acting in opposition to the basic life drive within us.

Perhaps this is a bit of a leap. But our feelings are the *ultimate* arbiter of what is right and wrong.

They come to us through prayer, meditation, or stillness. They are, in essence, our path or channel to God.

Self-Love comes First of All - When we allow the truth that we find in our deepest feelings to become the guiding force in our lives, we discover that indeed *I* am of paramount importance. The force of will, pressing us to stay in a hurtful place, is gradually replaced with the truth from our inner knowledge. We are obligated *above all* to care for ourselves.

This message comes very clear from inside. The depression, the frustration, the anger that our unhealthy relationships cause, all of these clamor for change. They are the feelings - the signals - that we are neglecting ourselves. And ultimately we must respect this obligation to ourselves, or we will perish. We will disappear as our spirits are pressed by abuse into smaller and smaller spaces, with greater and greater pain. Ultimately, our protection mechanisms will relieve this pain - by dissociation, by denial, by altered awareness, and ultimately by death.

Children need us - Last, many of us lose sight of the primary importance to our children of our own mental and spiritual health. We use our will to overcome the pain, resentment, and deprivation of our abusive and isolated lives to provide that intact family that we so value. Yet we lose sight of the damage that is done to us by this choice. We lose the balanced perspective we need to see how our parental interactions and parental models are diminished by the hurt we suffer and the abuse we allow.

Our first responsibility to our children is to be healthy ourselves. We would never choose to be physically unable to care for them. We have the same obligation to stay mentally and spiritually able to care for them. As nons we must *fight* for this well being. For many of us, it can only be found by leaving the relationship. If this is true, we are *obligated* to do this - to leave the relationship - if we are to provide the nurture and care that our children need.

The change doesn't have to be permanent. We can always come back. But we need to make sure that the right changes happen in our partner's behavior before we do that. And often, holding to a very serious boundary like this might be the only way to motivate a partner to make big changes.

On Changing Values

I've been asked how I managed to let go of the powerful sense of obligation that I held toward my "intact family" and my "marriage." I put these in quotes because they were fantasies - things that didn't really exist except in form. But nevertheless, viewed from outside the family, they certainly **appeared** to be there. And I know many nons struggle with strong values and obligations. So how **did** I make such a big change in my values?

Tears and Healing

To start, you need a model. My model is this: spirit; memory; cognition. The spirit is the true you, the essence of your life energy that drives toward what is true and good. It is also the guardian of your well being. Memory is the sum of your many experiences, and for most of us is loaded with all kinds of garbage that has nothing to do with our spirit, truth, or goodness. But, because it has been said or done to us, or thought by us, it *is* part of the base of knowledge and data by which we interpret our world and ourselves. Cognition is the thoughtful processing of sensory input against memory to produce conclusions or decisions.

Now, among the garbage in my memory were some things I took as absolute givens:

> Never, ever, *ever* get divorced;
>
> Above all else, children need an intact nuclear family;
>
> Don't ever look beyond your spouse for emotional support;
>
> Don't even *think* about having an affair;
>
> Act like people expect you to act;
>
> Above all, children *must* have a nuclear family.

OK, there was other stuff, but this was probably the key stuff.

So, there I was, cognitively processing the input from my world in the context of this memory

Chapter 6
Obligation – The Hook

bank. I was in an emotionally bankrupt relationship, and I knew it. I knew I needed and wanted more. This knowledge came from my spirit. But I was continuing to direct my life in accordance with my memory, the collection of rules and regulations, not to mention judgments, that dictated that I needed to stay in that relationship. Well, one thing I can tell you for sure: *when your memory is in conflict with your spirit, you are going to hurt*. Mostly this will manifest itself as depression. You can read more about this in Depression and Unconscious (p 68).

Notwithstanding that I was starting to feel lousy about life, starting to find myself crying or nearly so, these were very powerful strictures I had going. Now, how does one get past this?

I had some help from my spirit. Remember I said it guards your well being? It's not always good at this, but it tries. Well, my spirit was not too happy with me. Why? I was forcing myself to stay in an exclusive, abusive relationship. And if there's one thing that spirits don't like, it's abusive relationships. So mine said this: "Fine. You want to stay in that hellhole? OK. Stay. But while you're staying you're gonna do something for ME.

You see that pretty young thing over there? The one that's a little depressed, kind of like your wife? The one that's bright and pretty and sensitive, just like your wife? Yes, that's the one. Well, you've just got to have her. You can keep the witch if you insist. But you're going to *have* to go get someone else, too. Because we don't like it

119

down here in the dark, and we need some love and caring. And since you don't seem to think you need to get this from your marriage, you're just gonna have to go get that pretty little thing."

Now, if you've never been there, and I had never been there like *this* before, when your subconscious tells you that you *have* to do something, it doesn't play around. And mine went full power on me. These were among the most powerful feelings I have ever experienced. And they were not chosen. They did not follow from thoughts or conscious desires. They came directly from my unconscious mind. And if you're curious about "Why her?" have a look at my words on imago (p. 100). These feelings were so strong, they forced me to make changes. It was simply unbearable not to. (Just to be clear, there was no relationship. I never got anywhere close to her.)

Since at that time I did not have the understanding I needed to give *myself* permission to end my marriage, I was forced to seek another resolution. That motivation was overwhelming. And what ended up on the block were my strictures about seeking support, having a relationship outside of marriage, and being what others expected of me.

That was the end of givens number 3, 4, and 5. And when the whole mess was done (she, of course, was just as unhealthy as my wife was, and split me (p. 177) into an ax-murdering monster) numbers 1,2, and 6 had bitten the dust, too.

As for what I take as givens *now*, that would take another whole section, but I will say that children need, above all else, a safe, loving home and parent(s) who are as emotionally healthy as possible.

My life exploded, with help from my wife's alcoholism, NEC, depression, et cetera. But it was I who set the stage for such a fundamental change in my own values, by neglecting to care for myself when the signals were clearly there that I needed more than I was getting. I don't commend this to you, but this is how my sense of obligation and my belief system changed.

Tears and Healing

Chapter 7
Healing the Abuse

Healing Takes Work

Of all the tasks that we face in emerging from an abusive relationship, healing the damage of abuse is the most difficult and the task that inevitably takes the longest. Our finances can be rebuilt; our emotions will rebound; new friends can be made; new partners found.

But those anguishing memories – those painful thoughts about ourselves – these are difficult to escape.

It can be done. But it takes time. And it takes work, and a determination to heal.

But let's be honest. Safety is a prerequisite. There is no way we can undo the damage from abuse that is still going on. We cannot hope to save ourselves from damage that we at the same time are continuing to accept.

If you are still in an abusive situation, read on. I hope it will empower you. Certainly you can do some good for yourself, whatever your circumstance. But if your goal is to heal, to be happy, to fulfill your potential in life, to become all you can become... then you will have to free yourself from the abuse.

In the next few pages, I'll explain how I envision our minds working. Then I'll explain how verbal abuse sets our minds against us, and the pain that results. Finally, I'll tell you how I think we can work to heal that damage. The last page talks about how our spirit helps to guide us towards areas of our lives that we haven't properly nurtured, and the role that tears (oh, so many tears) play in our healing.

Memory Shapes Us

The great thing about waxing philosophic about how the mind works is that no one can ever prove that you're wrong. Well, let's admit up front that the mind is a pretty complicated thing. I'm not trying to explain everything that happens in our minds. Specifically, I'm going to talk about two extremes that I have experienced: the aftermath of intense and prolonged verbal abuse on the one hand, and the approaching and striving for the ideal self on the other hand.

What I'll say here is based on a model: a way of thinking about how our experiences combine with our life energy and our thought processes to shape what we do and what we feel. Now, if I were a real hard-core techie, I would be writing mathematical equations down. But I'll spare you the mathematics. I'm only going to talk in general terms.

Three Part Model

The model that has helped me deal with my own abusive experiences has three parts. As you read this, keep in mind that the purpose of a model is give us a mechanism describing how something works so that we can predict how things *will* work in a given situation. The test of a model is how well it helps us to deal with situations we couldn't otherwise understand.

Spirit: The first part, down in my chest, just below the sternum, is where I feel my life energy. This is where I physically feel my life energy, and where I physically feel my deepest and least cognitive feelings. When I'm really moved to do something, I feel it here. When something is really wrong, I feel that here. I prefer for myself to refer to this energy as my **spirit**.

Thought: The second part of my model I feel in my head, mostly around my temples and behind my eyes. This is where I sense the activity of my rational thought. This is where, when I am struggling to comprehend something, I feel the tension and the energy build. This is where the wheels turn. The second part of my model is **thought or cognition**.

Memory: So far I described two components, but without any context. It is the third component that provides this. It is this component that provides the basis of knowledge and understanding for thoughts. And also provides the impression of the world within which our spirit must live and function. This third part is our **memory**. Our spirit is an energy and definition that we are born with. Our thinking is really a process that we can direct but not really control. But our memory is something that we and others can freely, and sometimes destructively, manipulate. Memory is not something I physically feel, but when I relate it to my spirit and my thoughts, I like to envision it as a layer or barrier between my head, where my thoughts are, and my chest, where my spirit resides.

Memory ⇔ Spirit

Now let me talk a little about how these interact. Bear with me here, because until I explain how these interplay, I really can't get to how this affects us. Let's start by looking at how memory interacts with the spirit.

Spirit Drives our Lives: I believe that our spirit is the essential driving force toward what we are supposed to be in this life. It is a phenomenally energizing source, and it also contains within it a complete definition of what is moral and good. If you are a Christian (for example), this energy and vision of right and wrong is what you might interpret as God's will expressed in answer to prayer. The energizing power that comes from our spirit could be interpreted as God's love for us. I believe that our spirits are unique, and each of us is called to some unique role in this world by our spirit.

Our spirit's job, then, is to direct our lives in a way consistent with our unique calling. And I believe it can do this in one of two ways.

First Role: First of all, when we are in a reasonably healthy state of mind, our spirits energize us with visions of greater things for ourselves, which lead us toward our unique calling. As an example, as I worked myself up from the depths of despair and abuse, I discovered that part of my calling in this world is to speak to others about healing and growth (which is exactly what I'm doing right now). Trust me when I tell you that this was never something that my cognitive processes would have remotely suggested to me. When we are safe, healthy, and relaxed, our spirit becomes free to empower us and guide us toward the things that we should be doing and our lives.

Second Role: The second function that our spirit performs is to act as guardian of our life calling. And this is where memory comes into play. Our spirit is not in direct connection with either our thoughts or our sensory perceptions. It does not know what is around us in our world. Our spirit is completely enveloped within our memory. Its only understanding of what is happening in our lives comes from what we remember.

When our memories are in harmony with the direction our spirit leads us, we feel good. In this state, our spirit can erupt with a wonderful, energizing flow of vision, motivation, and fulfilling emotions. But when our memories are in conflict with the direction of our spirit, we become ill. We become distressed. We become depressed and physically sick. Peck (p. 165) talks about this, which I described in Depression and the Unconscious (p. 68), but he doesn't talk about the role of memory, so his model is somewhat different. And I believe that when our spirit becomes busy sounding the alarm in this way, it is unable at the same time to energize us toward the positive things it seeks for us in life.

Memory ⇔Thought

Now let's talk about how memory interacts with our thoughts.

First Way: Like the spirit, our thought processes operate in the context of our memories. Our memories are where our knowledge and understanding of the world is maintained. Our thoughts also are in direct connection with the perceptions of our senses. By senses I mean not just raw sight, sound, smell, etc., but also more complete perceptions such as the understanding of things that are spoken to us or the meaning of images or scenes that we see, for example. As sensory input is received, we process that by thinking about it, and the way we think about it is determined by what we have kept in our memory.

Just to give a simple example, if a two-year old sees a porcupine for the first time, the child's reaction may be, "Oh, a small furry animal. Good to pet. I will pet it." This is based on the child's memory of other small animals, which are good to pet. I, on the other hand, with my more complete memory, which includes memories of porcupines, see the same animal and know to steer clear. So one type of interaction between thought and memory is the processing of sensory input in the context of our memory.

Second Way: There is however, the second way that thought interacts with memory. We can allow our thoughts to pass without retaining them, but if we choose, we can add to our memory from our thought processes. The simplest case of this is when we choose to remember something. Unfortunately, there is another way for things to get into our memory. If we feel or think an experience is important, it is likely to be impressed into our memory. If I start to step out into the street in front of a car and catch myself at the last second from certain death, I am likely to remember that. So too, if I see an athlete I greatly admire win an Olympic medal, I'm likely to remember that. If someone walked up to me on the street and shouted in my face that I had stolen his wallet, I would probably remember that, too. And if my wife screams at me that I am a pervert and a pedophile and not fit to be a father, well, yes. I do remember that. Indeed.

You see, when we allow someone into our intimate personal space, especially if that intimacy is kept for a long time, then most everything that person says is going to be important. If those things are not true, we still remember them. And they become part of our memory.

Memory is Finite: Now, our memory is not an unbounded thing. The things that we knew or believed in the past can be replaced in our memory by new experiences. Let's say, for example, that as a young adult I found that I was not very much of a people person. So my memory, which shapes both my thoughts and influences my spirit, has filled this memory space labeled "people person" with a dis-association with me. Later in my life, I might discover that I am able to help people in support communities, and people find me compassionate and inspiring, and that I feel energized and feel good about this. And over time, these experiences, which seem important to me, gradually overwrite that memory, so that I now have this memory space labeled "people person" filled with a positive association with myself. The old memories have been displaced by the new. You could call this learning or even re-learning.

Effects of Verbal Abuse

Abuse Overwhelms Our Memory: Now with this, we can begin to understand what verbal abuse does to us. Some people will say and even honestly feel, "I can deal with this. I'm an adult. I know these abusive statements are not true." But unfortunately, I don't believe we have the power to deal with such abuse. Because when we are verbally abused, and hurtful untruths about us are told to us, often in the most forceful way, it IS important. And it IS retained in our memory. And if it goes on, it will eventually overwhelm our truthful memories and leave us with a memory system that is filled with hurtful, hateful lies. And this is the essence of how we are damaged by verbal abuse.

What does this mean? What does it mean if our memories are filled with lies; with vicious destructive untruths that demean us? Perhaps you might think, "So what if I remember that? I KNOW that those things aren't true. Why should they concern me?" And indeed, I believe that I probably thought such a thing myself at one point. But they do concern us. Remember, our memory is the context in which our cognitive thought processes operate, and it also provides the only perspective on the outside world to our spirit.

So, two things are going to happen.

Thoughts Are Distorted: First, we begin to think irrationally – unrealistically - about ourselves. When we need to think about ourselves, our thought processes automatically refer to our memory for context. If my memory is filled with the concept that I am a pervert and an unfit father, no matter how untrue, my thoughts are directed and affected by these memories. It is impossible for me to think about myself without bringing the abusive lies in my memory into play. My thoughts are thus distorted, and the conclusions resulting from my thoughts reflect the negative, ugly lies embedded in my memory. No matter how much I might deny the reality of the lies, they become part of how I see and think about myself. My thoughts are no longer balanced and realistic. And what is worse, these distorted thoughts can reinforce the lies in my memory and make the damage even worse.

Our Spirit Is Violated: The second thing that happens comes from our spirit. Remember, our spirit is enveloped in a world view provided by our memory. The energy of our spirit drives us toward goodness and fulfillment of our life calling. And when my spirit finds itself immersed in a view of myself that I am a pervert and an unfit father, it takes issue with this. It does not like this state of affairs. And it makes this known with emotional distress. It may take the form of depression (as I described in Depression and the Unconscious, p. 68), or anxiety, and it may also make itself felt physically. Physical symptoms might be stress headaches, hypertension, hyperacidity, and in more severe situations, nausea, diarrhea, and vomiting. Verbal abuse makes us sick.

Recap

In other sections I will talk more about how we can reverse the damage from verbal abuse. But to close this section, let me just reiterate the basic concepts in this model. Our spirit is our life energy and directs us to positive and healthy choices that realize our unique life calling. Our thoughts and cognitions are the mental processes by which we process sensory input to make conclusions and choose actions. Our memory is the sum of our experiences, either events which are important or which we have chosen to remember.

Chapter 7
Healing the Abuse

Our spirit knows only the world reflected by our memory. When our memory conflicts with the drives of our spirit, our spirit opposes this by sickening us with depression, anxiety, and physical distress. When our memory is in harmony with the spirit, our spirit energizes us and leads us to new and better choices in life. Our thoughts operate in the context of our memory, which defines how we process the input we receive.

When we are verbally abused, the attacks are important enough that they are embedded in our memory. If the abuse persists long enough, the abusive assertions overwrite our truthful, realistic impressions of ourselves, and leave us with a memory that defines us in demeaning, negative, and hurtful ways. This impression conflicts with the positive life energy of our spirit, and as a result our spirit signals that something is wrong with depression, anxiety, and physical illness.

Now To Do Something

Now, please bear in mind that I am not trying to build an anatomically correct model of our bodies. I am not presuming to enable a surgeon to correct verbal abuse by excising some particular item of anatomy. What I want to do here is to build an understanding, in a way you can relate to, of how you can help yourself to heal from your verbally abusive experiences. Because I believe you can undo the damage of hateful words, and there are definite actions you can take to bring that to pass.

Healing Abuse -
Building Faith in Ourselves

In the previous section, I described the critical role that memory plays in how we think about ourselves, and how our spirit's energy is focused. When verbal abuse fills our memory with hateful lies, our spirit sickens us with depression and stress, and our thoughts about ourselves become distorted. If the abuse is severe and prolonged, we can even lose touch with the reality of what we really are and begin to believe the abusive lies. This is brainwashing, a subject that, not surprisingly, I wrote about when I was in the throes of abuse.

It is a tough road to heal this damage, but it can be done. In fact, I believe that if we make ourselves safe from abuse and adopt some simple habits, in time we can completely erase the effect on our thoughts and our spirit.

Stop the Music

Remember that our memory is the product of a flow of ideas coming in, and the loss of older, different ideas. Well, before we can make any serious progress on filling our memory with the right stuff, we have to stop the hurtful lies that we've been subjected to. Otherwise it just becomes a competition. And competing with the anger and vehemence of a verbally abusive partner is a losing proposition. My STBX, at her worst, would escalate and escalate with more and more energy and ugliness until she achieved the control she wanted. It will help to push back against this with positive messages, but it is impossible to heal in the face of it. So first and foremost, for healing to really work, we have to be safe from verbal abuse.

It Is All About Reprogramming

Remember that our memory is a cumulative, but limited storage. It represents our recent experiences most strongly but it also represents some older experiences. As experiences become very old, they are displaced by newer ones. This is how abuse overcomes our reasonable knowledge of ourselves. It simply floods our memory with lies. Eventually the lies start to make up a significant part of our view of ourselves.

Reprogramming: We can heal the affects of verbal abuse in exactly the same way that the abuse damaged us: by loading our memory with truth. I said that memories are formed when we choose to remember, and also when experiences are important. The key element, I believe, in both these routes is **belief**. The experience, whether something said to us, something we think, or something we perceive from the actions of another person, have to represent something we believe.

So to undo this damage, we need to embark on a sustained program of stuffing truth into our heads! Simple! But.... HOW??

Starting From a Bad Place : The problem, when we are in the throes of abuse, or recently emerged from sustained abuse, is that we have lost faith in ourselves. We have been brainwashed, and have accepted the lies and now see ourselves, at least partly, as those lies define us. Just trying to think "I am not a selfish, hateful person," we probably wouldn't make much progress because we have come to believe the lies, and therefore this message is rejected before it can get into our memory. Even though we *think* that we are not selfish or hateful, we have lost faith and we don't really **believe** that this is true. Without belief, it is hard to impress the statement into our memory. We need some kind of jump-start to get some input into us that rebuilds some of that faith.

Support Communities Build Faith: I talked about how helpful support communities are when we are just getting started with a healing process. This is because the communities resonate with faith. When we screw up our courage and raise our heads in a support group, we are embraced with faith. People that we don't (yet) know assure us with perfect confidence that we *are* good people. And their faith in us can be the jump start that gets us out of a terribly stuck place. This could also come from healthy, supportive family, or even from therapy. But I think it would take a lot of therapy to deal with the impact of sustained verbal abuse.

If you have never participated in a support list, you should. Support lists surround you with people who have been where you are; who have walked in your shoes; and can truly understand your anguish. Whatever your concern, whatever hurts, whatever you stumble over, someone is there to reassure and encourage. It is, in Peck's lingo, an expression of "grace".

Tears and Healing

I don't know about you, but I've shed plenty of tears on this long road. And I think I've finally figured out how this works.

Spirit/Mind I go back again to Peck (p. 165). He teaches that depression results from a disconnect between our conscious and our unconscious minds. I'll take some liberty with this and put it another way. The problem is a disconnect between our *spirit* and our *mind.* Your spirit is you - it is the complete, full, good and healthy you. It is the vital energy that drives your life. It is the source of joy and inspiration. Your memory, on the other hand, is programmable. In an abusive relationship, it can become a garbage can stuffed full of thoughts that have been shoved in there by you and the people you've been around. And when I say garbage, for those of us in long term relationships with abusive partners, I *mean* garbage.

You see, we may think we know what we think, but I realize now that's not so. What we think is a conglomerate of all the stuff that's been said and done to us. I might sit here and say to you, "I know I'm a faithful husband." And you would think that means that I think I'm a faithful husband. But not so fast.

I had somebody helping to shape these thoughts about me - an abusive spouse. And she told me over and over, in a pretty violent way, that I was NOT faithful to her. My reason and logic says "I've never done anything unfaithful." But that's not what I think. The doubt has crept in, and what I really think is that I'm not sure if I'm a faithful husband.

Now, my spirit tells me that I'm faithful, and moves me to be faithful. But my mind, now polluted with thoughts stuffed into it by an abusive spouse, isn't sure. This disconnect is going to cause problems. If it's important to me, it's going to make me depressed. I'm going to feel bad about myself, have less energy and initiative, and feel the other manifestations of depression. Now bear with me because I haven't gotten to the tears yet.

Follow the unfaithful example along a bit further. Let's say I'm feeling depressed about this. And I have a chance to talk with one of my close friends. I don't really know I'm depressed about this, because I think I know what I'm thinking (that I'm faithful), so I don't know to ask for help with it. But I do know that I'm sick of hearing this from my spouse. And when I mention it to my friend, the first words that come back are "Of course you've been faithful." And suddenly I'm holding back tears.

Tears Come When You Release the Conflict - What triggered the tears was a change in my thoughts. Someone said something that helps to reverse the conflict between my spirit (I'm faithful and want to be) and my thoughts (I'm not sure

Chapter 7
Healing the Abuse

because my abusive spouse tells me over and over I'm not). It unwinds some of the thought training that caused the conflict.

Think about your own experiences. Surely you can remember times when a friend or family member has reassured you about some aspect of yourself around which you've been attacked. And you have this upwelling of tears. It certainly has been consistent in my life.

Tears Are Leading You to Your Whole Self - So tears, in effect, are pointing out the path to freeing your whole self. When you well up, think about what positive affirmation you've just received. This is an area where you need more *conscious* work, *thought* work, to retrain your memory to match your spirit. And I can guarantee that the retraining means shoving positive thoughts into your mind - into your memory bank of experience.

This is the learning for me. It happens a lot to me, because my wife has attacked my character in every imaginable way. And she has shoved a tremendous amount of ***garbage,*** and I mean garbage, into my memory. I'm learning now to give up the "I know I'm a good person" routine. Logic doesn't cut it. It's experience that defines what we know, and abusive experiences load us with garbage about ourselves. I know now, from being aware of my tears, that I'm really not sure if I'm faithful, and I need to get some input on that. Over and over. Because she's abused me over and over. And it isn't going to go away with one little reassurance.

Pay Attention to the Message - The other learning is that, if tears are signaling me, I need to deal with that issue. I might not like it, but I need to. Because it's about a violation of my spirit. This is where a lot of nons could learn more about why they're unhappy with their relationships or their situations. Let's say I'm being given a thought about divorcing my wife and finding someone else that can smile and be happy with me, and it's making me cry. I better think about that. Because my spirit is calling for something. The thoughts in the garbage can are saying "I won't leave my wife." But the spirit is making itself felt. It needs more. I need more. I need a relationship in which I'm loved and valued, not degraded. There's no point in dodging it. And antidepressants won't make that go way.

Let me give another example; something has come to me recently. I pretty much admit to being an emotional teenager, so it should be no surprise I listen to a lot of popular music. Lately I've been having some pretty strong emotional reactions to songs that deal with gratitude and complete, balanced relationships. This was a tricky one. I know enough now that when I'm welling up, there is a message there I need to find. But I kept thinking that I wanted to fall in love, or I wanted to be in love again. That doesn't really fit what I know about myself right now, so I kept pondering this. And finally, I got an insight that I think explains the message.

Chapter 7
Healing the Abuse

These songs are about gratitude for complete relationships. And the insight here is that there is an aspect of me that I think is pretty important that has never been validated. I'm a very **giving** person. And even in the face of miserable NEC behavior, I gave my wife a lot of love and care. The problem is simple: **she couldn't acknowledge or appreciate what I gave her**. So the learning here is simple: find a relationship with someone who can accept, appreciate and acknowledge my love. Wow. Sounds simple. But it took some determination for me to ferret that out.

Tears - they tell us so much about where we need to go. They are the guiding lights of recovery. To follow that guide, it will take help from others and courage. But that is the path to wholeness, to true satisfaction - the path to the light.

Tears and Healing

Chapter 8
Moving on

On Seeking Permission

Most everyone takes marriage vows very seriously. It is ingrained in us all our lives to see them as the most sacred of promises. And most nons hold their promise to their spouse as their highest commitment.

Unfortunately for some, the pain of the relationship truly tests this commitment. When things reach the point where vows are pulling in one direction, and our need for safety and sanity pulls in the opposite direction, it's time to seek a higher perspective. Everybody sees this a little differently, but you need to connect with your highest authority, and seek the most fundamental answer to the question: Is what you are doing wrong?

Our obligation to our spouses is but one obligation among many we have. We also have sacred obligations to nurture our children and even to love ourselves. To nurture our children, we must ourselves be whole and functioning. What are we to do when our commitment to our marriage jeopardizes our ability to fulfill our commitment to our children? This is especially critical for those nons whose spouses are partly or totally unable to provide nurturing for their children. If not us, then who? Can we allow the illness of a spouse to put our children's care in jeopardy?

Seeking Permission

For many nons, the situation boils down to a choice: either we keep our commitment to our spouse and lose our own peace, and possibly even the ability to care for our children; or we choose to step outside the bounds we have set in our marriage commitments, and take care of ourselves and our children first. Most of us have a very difficult time accepting the second choice. And ultimately, to do so, we need to be granted permission to step outside the bounds of our vows.

For those with strong belief in God, this can be found by seeking God's will. This will come through prayer, reflection, and scripture. We need to ask whether God intends for us to suffer in this way, or whether He instead grants us permission to care for ourselves and our children, in the face of terrible pain, by stepping outside those vows.

For me, I find this authority within myself. I believe that my spirit ultimately defines truth and right. I sought, through meditation and reflection, to connect with those most basic feelings. When I did, I found that I was freely granted the right to

do what was right for me, to say NO to the hurtful
behavior, and to do things I thought others would
disapprove of. But in fact, no one disapproved.
Ultimately, the choices I made were accepted by
those around me.

If you allow yourself to second guess what others
are saying and thinking about you, you will almost
certainly feel bad about your choices, or worse.
Remember, they don't know the reality; they don't
know how sick your spouse is. In fact they
probably have false data based on the "ideal"
behavior that many disturbed spouses show in
public.

You may find your highest authority through
prayer, scripture, meditation, or any other way that
works for you. Only you and your highest
authority can truly assess your actions, grant you
permission, and bless your choices. For many of
us, this is a task of primary importance.

Overcoming Fear

Well, it's one thing to think about making changes
in your life. Or even to decide that we need to
make changes. But the real kicker comes when it's
time to actually make those changes happen. And
that, my friend, is where all of us run smack into
fear. And it can be paralyzing, totally paralyzing.

Ignorance Guards Fear

This fear is protected with a wall of ignorance.
Take divorce: Can I make a living? Is it best for

the children? Can I get custody? Partial custody? How much alimony will she/he/I get? How long will it take? Can I afford the fight? And so on.

All these questions have answers, or approximate answers. And it's pretty certain that if we're feeling afraid, we probably don't know these answers. These answers give you the understanding and knowledge to allow you to see where change will take you. The more of the answers you have, the less ignorance you have to protect your fears. Once the fears diminish, it becomes possible to make the decision WITHOUT anguish. What's more, it becomes emotionally possible to start making those changes.

Fear is dealt with by 1000 tiny steps to LEARN. It's amazing how little we know about the things we fear. One phone call, a visit to a web site, a phone call to a friend, a question on a support list - can provide the knowledge to change something from a fearful unknown to "Hey! I can do that!" The key is to recognize the fear of change, and put your finger on what you are assuming, without really knowing, that makes you afraid. From that, you can take a step to get a better understanding. And once you have it, you'll be able to take another step.

It may take ten or 20 small steps to make a big change. For me, a great example was finding a divorce attorney. I was so frightened of that. But I did the 20 steps, one by one: buy a book; read the book; look in the phone book; read the book again; talk to a friend; read that book again to find

out what I'm supposed to ask; make a list of
questions; write a script for a voicemail; look on
the internet; look again; try harder this time; make
a call; return a call, make an appointment; Every
damned one of those things I was afraid of. Even
buying the book! I bought it with cash so my wife
wouldn't ask what I'd bought! But as a result of
those small steps, I was able to make a big change.

Once I determined to knock these walls down,
everything came into focus and my actions
became part of a plan. Something that I chose and
I took control of. By eliminating ignorance of the
"what ifs", you eliminate the anguish and allow
yourself to own your choices, and to move
forward and change your life.

Step by step, little by little, you knock down the
walls of ignorance that guard those fears.

Limits of Faith

Well, I have preached at the men on the support
lists enough about hanging in too long. When
relationships get really bad, they drain us. And
while we all want to be faithful to our
relationships, we can really get ourselves in a bind
by sticking with a harmful situation so long that
we don't have the strength left to salvage
ourselves. And it's not just men that this can
happen to - it's just that men's situations are closer
to my experience so I identify with it more.

We ALL are, or have been, faithful to our relationships. But it is really important to be realistic about our own strength. By staying in the relationship as the primary concern in our lives, we put ourselves at risk of becoming exhausted and non-functional. You're not reading this to celebrate your wedded bliss. We all need to be pragmatic and recognize that exiting the relationship is a real possibility. When things get really bad, it has to be considered.

The problem is that exiting is *hard*. It's important not to exhaust yourself being faithful for so long that you don't have enough strength left to manage that difficult transition - *if* it comes. We all should have an emotional rainy day fund that we can draw on if we need to leave. Repeated upheavals and crises are exhausting – *even if* we manage to get through them. I felt like I was managing just fine almost until the point I realized I *had* to get out of my relationship. But I barely kept it together through the eight months between my decision to divorce and the point where she moved out. It was a painful time. And that was *after* I gave up.

Don't go there. Even if you *really* want your relationship to work, keep something in reserve. It's a reasonable enough thing to do.

Cutting Your Losses, or Maximizing Your Gains?

I hear a pretty consistent theme in the comments from nons who are in long term relationships. The idea is that things are tolerable; things are ok; or they're not ok but if the spouse makes progress in therapy then things will be manageable. Nobody is ever happy.

The question that needs to be asked here is a simple one: What do you want your life to be? Do you want to keep working on and on to cut your losses and keep the situation bearable? Or do you want to take a new path, pay off those emotional debts, and start making something positive in your life?

Not that simple, though, huh? It's not. It's a daunting question. But I guarantee, if you don't work hard to answer it, you'll never get the answer. You'll stay where you are, stay unhappy, and each day you'll make a deposit of your life's energy into an account that runs the real risk of never having a positive balance.

Answering Those Downside Questions

There are *so many* reasons not to change. It will be bad for the children. I will lose custody of the children. It will cost too much. I don't have a job. I would have to move. I would have to pay alimony. My spouse will fight me. I'm afraid he'll hurt me. And on.

The first thing you need to realize here is that, for the most part, you ***don't know*** what the outcome of these things will be. You are sitting in ignorance about what your future choices are. And because you don't know, you feel afraid. And

because you're afraid, you don't do anything - like
a deer caught in the headlights.

So, whether you are determined to stay, or just
don't know what is the right thing to do, you owe
it to yourself to fill in these gaping holes of
ignorance about your options. How can you truly
choose to stay if you don't know what other
choices you have? So you need to do some hard
work. Let's look at some of these issues:

- **It's bad for the kids**. Are you sure? What
  would it be like? What is it like now? How
  dysfunctional is your home? How badly
  are you affected by your spouse's illness?
  How much more could you give your
  children in your own safe home? How safe
  are your children? How safe do they feel?
  What do you know about children who live
  with both parents? Have you discussed this
  with a counselor or therapist? Chances are,
  if you're here reading this, your children
  live in a home that hurts. You, as their one
  healthy parent, owe it to them to find out
  the answers to these questions. Have a look
  at the section on Staying for the Kids (p.
  111).

- **I will lose custody of the children**. Will
  you? Are you an active parent? Do you
  stay close to your children? How does your
  spouse's behavior affect them? Has he/she
  been hospitalized? Have a record of
  behavior problems? What are the laws and
  customs in your state and county? Have
  you consulted an attorney? The reality is

that you don't know until you really dig
into it. Don't assume you lose. I didn't. I
worked the hard stuff and I made it work
for me. You might be able to do the same.

- **It will cost too much**. Well, this is a
  problem. But it doesn't have to stop you.
  You need money for attorneys. You might
  need money for psych testing. But you're
  living somehow now. If your spouse has
  income, do you know how you can get it?
  Do you know what the laws and customs
  are for support? In my state, if you file for
  divorce and live apart, you are entitled to
  support. If you live apart and have
  children, you are entitled to support. Well,
  it's not nice. But then, what are you living
  with now? Consult an attorney. If you
  really can't afford one, or can't pay safely,
  seek free counsel. Legal aid societies will
  provide this.

- **I don't have a job**. Another problem. But
  presumably you can deal with this. Is it
  real, or is it just a good reason to sit still?

- **I would have to move**. This isn't nice. But
  then, how was yesterday for you?

- **I would have to pay alimony**. You might.
  I have to. And you might be able to survive
  it. Have to change the way you live?
  Maybe. Is it worth it? How can you know
  if you don't know what kind of alimony
  and/or child support you'd be obligated

for? An attorney can give you a sense of this.

- **My spouse will fight me.** Same old same old. You deal with it now, don't you?

- **I'm afraid he'll hurt me.** This is serious. But, are you afraid now? Probably. Have you sought protection? Shouldn't you? Is this how you want to live? Is this love? Is this caring? Whether you stay or go, you need to deal with violence. You just cannot stay on in a physically unsafe situation. Contact a local domestic violence hotline. Ask for help. Call the local police, explain, and ask for help. If your SO hurts you, call 911. This one is important. Protect yourself no matter what you do for the future.

What About the Upside?

If you stay, you fight and fight to keep your losses down. Things hurt, your needs aren't met. You are squashed.

What if you take a new direction? What if you say "No more!" to a partner who can't care for you? How many times have you longed for a partner who could genuinely smile at you? Someone who actually cared about your feelings? Someone who you can disagree with and still be happy? Someone who could - God forbid - **love** you? Time to go read the page on Love vs. In-Love (p. 89).

There is another world that can be found. It may not be easy, it may not come fast. But when you

Chapter 8
Moving on

stop the madness you give yourself the chance to reach for the sky. But only you can extend that reach. Only you can make the choice to grow. Only you can stop losing and start working to win in your life.

Tears and Healing

Chapter 9
After the Dawn

It seems like it will never end… the anguish and the insanity and the tangled web of involvement.

But there is life after; it is just different than what we have had before. In some ways it feels empty, but in other ways it is richer than you might have dared to imagine.

This section is no more than a few of my reflections on my life after the dark clouds parted.

A Touch of Grace

I wrote this about 16 months after my separation and about two years after I resolved to divorce my troubled wife.

Some days better.

Not all my days are joyful. But some are.

Today I was graced.

Tears and Healing

Today I was graced with a morning in which I did not have to get up early and go to work.

Today I was graced with a body that did not hurt.

Today I was graced with enough insight to answer my homework, and a fast internet connection to do it with.

Today I was graced with the time to work out as long as I wanted, and with the stamina to go for an hour and 45 minutes.

Today I was graced with a body, all of whose parts worked, and legs that weren't tired.

Today I was graced with the face of an old friend and coach.

Today I was graced with a feeling of success.

Today I was graced with the task of driving my new car for two hours, and with a stereo that turns music into motion.

Today I was graced with a trip with no snags, no hang-ups, and no delays.

Today I was graced with the reminder, in the form of the company of a lovely lady, captive in the seat beside me, that there is someone out there for me.

Today I was graced with confidence in myself, and the patience to reflect on the many gifts I have received.

Chapter 9
After the Dawn

Just Being Me

As strange it would have seemed just two or three years ago, my children now spend half their time with their mom and half with me. This includes some strange shuttling around holidays. This was written on Christmas Eve, about 18 months after I separated.

I was driving home earlier, after I dropped my girls at their mom's for the night. Snow was falling, the night was quiet, I was listening to whatever I wanted to without worrying about who would say what.

Tears were rolling down my face on the way over with the girls. I forget what I was thinking. It doesn't matter. My life is peaceful. My children are free of anger and anguish. I have bright hopes for new relationships.

I was just plain being me; being what I should be.

I wish I could remember what that special post was about. Something about how it is now and how it used to be. Life is different than I ever thought it would be. Different, and better. I am slowly learning to put down the crosses, cut the albatrosses loose, and live life now. It seems to work. I think I am alive.

I still remember the pain. Even before it got bad, it was crushing. Then it tried to consume me, and nearly did. But it is gone now. I went out at 10:00 PM on Christmas Eve and strung some more lights in the tree out front. Why? Who cares? I wanted to and there was no one to flare at me; no one to demean me; no one to tell me how horrid such a thing would be. They look nice, too. But that's beside the point.

I still have lots of tears. Every day. Sometimes it is not very convenient. But they come without pain now. They are those silent signals of healing. I know now what they mean. Usually I know what they're about too: validation. Reclaiming me, in all my glory, in all my insignificance.

I used to write about the damage of abuse. How it overwhelms your understanding; fills your memory with vicious lies. There is no fix but to replace each and every hurtful word with a truthful one; with one that redeems the lost part of us. So I know how deep those wounds are. Still healing, after so long; healing every day.

I like myself today. I am proud of what I am. I am proud of what I have done. I am proud of the courage it took to protect myself, and the hurt I suffered to protect my children.

My holiday this year is full of peace and contentment. I wish for each one of you to find the same, down whatever path, in whatever way works for you. Now I think I will go act my age and listen to Christina Aguilera. I'm just learning how to live, after all.

Tears Without Pain

The tears come without pain now – there is no wrench in the gut; no wish that it would stop. Yes, we do cry when hurt – or is not until after that we cry – when someone comforts us or we comfort ourselves?

The tears signal healing – they tell us that what we are thinking, feeling, hearing, seeing, imagining, smelling, touching – whatever the experience is – is healing for us. For me this always matches up to

Chapter 9
After the Dawn

correcting something that was said or done to me in senseless anger. At first it was something as blunt as saying out loud to myself "you are not a pervert." This was hard at first. Later when I honored feelings that I had been forced to suppress, by, for example, buying music that I liked, I started experiencing it with healthy actions. Now I recognize that just being aware that I'm in a comfortable and safe place registers as healing. Something so basic – one of the first things swept away by the abuse.

All of these things carry a message to my spirit. All of them correct hateful messages that I was accosted with. All of them validate what I am. They are all self-loving.

Back when I was fighting "I am not a pervert," there was pain. Now there is no pain. The situation is peaceful, fulfilling. The tears tell me I am still healing; still in the process of redeeming myself. I don't know when it will end, but I think it will end. I think there will come a time when I've kept myself from that kind of harm, and cared enough for myself that the healing will be over. Then, I expect a life without constant tears.

But I welcome the tears. They are like a compass – they tell me I am on the right path – like the pole star.

Here are some words that resonate for me. Read them and see if they do anything:

Tears and Healing

Will you give up, give in
When your heart's crying out "That
is wrong!"
Will you love you for you at the
end of it all?

Now in life there's gonna be times
When you're feeling low
And in your mind insecurities seem
to take control.
We start to look outside ourselves
For acceptance and approval
We keep forgetting that the one
thing we should know is:

Don't be scared
To fly alone
Find a path that is your own
Love will open every door.

[From *Stripped*, by Christina Aguilera, Rob
Hoffman and Heather Holley]

If this makes you well up or cry or want to cry,
there is a message.

The message is: you are looking outside for
something that can only be found within. You are
being something that is not you. These words
resonate because they express the feeling and
motivation of your spirit. They resonate because
they validate that YOU must be YOU, not what
other people think you should be. They stand up
and shout for your spirit to be expressed in your
life and in your choices.

I don't know about you, but being me is hard. I'm different – and not always in ways that people can appreciate. It's scary – to go out in the world being just me. But I have realized there is no other way for me to live MY life. To be MY life it has to be MINE; not someone else's. So I gingerly stick my toes out into new places, and somehow I find that no one has chopped them off; if anything it has allowed me to be closer to people.

Music is a powerful connector to our spiritual energy. It moves us when it resonates with what we are inside. These are important messages that we need to listen to, and do our best to honor.

The Clouds Part

Wow.

It has been two years since I handed my wife's problems back to her and informed her that we would be co-parenting our children in separate lives. I endured a firestorm of abuse until she found another home and moved out six months later.

The good news is that she stepped up to taking care of her life. It was rocky for a while, unstable, and unpleasant for me, but it's now clear that she did begin to move her life in the right direction. Today, after 18 months apart, she has made enough progress that I will no longer be barbing her with comic acronyms –though these helped me through difficult times. From here on I'll refer to her as my STBXW, and hopefully soon my XW.

About eight weeks ago she was victimized yet again, this time by a surgeon who nearly killed her with a gross error. The difficult recovery had a silver lining, however. In the course of dealing with the suffering and injury, she became aware of something she called "the black and white thinking," and she went on to say that once she recognized it, she could start to deal with it. The black clouds of denial part, and the sun peeks through at last.

I don't know what the quality of her life is now. I think she has friends through AA with whom she is at least partly her real self. She continues to be a fine parent and our children are thriving. She no longer seems interested in changing the custody arrangement, and the children are much more at ease with it. But there is no doubt in my mind that her improvement hinged on my thrusting her out into the cold world. As long as she had me and the family unit to compensate for her problems, I believe her avoidance of responsibility would have continued. And so, as destructive and costly as divorce is, I think in this case it served a virtuous purpose.

May those black clouds never return.

Chapter 10
Resources

Books

Better get used to reading, because recovery takes
a lot of it. And if you're still with your BPSO,
you'll need a safe place to stash these books where
they won't be seen!

If this list is too short for you, have a look at the
compilation of everything I've read along my road
to healing in My Recovery Library.

Stop Walking on Eggshells – by Mason and
Kreger - If you are involved with someone with
borderline personality disorder or its behaviors,
this is a definitive book. It explains BP behavior
and how it affects those around the BP. It teaches
boundaries and coping techniques. If your SO is
BP, you should definitely read this.

Getting the Love You Want, and ***Keeping the
Love you Find*** - by Harville Hendrix - Either of
these books will help you understand what is
happening to you when you are in love - and I

mean "head over heals," "out of your mind," "can't live without him/her." Falling in love is probably the most dangerous thing a non can do. Learn about it to escape its evil spell.

The Road Less Traveled - by M. Scott Peck - a classic book on spirituality and mental health. Use this book to understand what your spirit is telling you, and understand why you hurt so much. This book led me out of despair and into change

Codependent No More - by Melody Beattie – this book did not work for me, because it's written from the perspective of recovery from addiction, but it's a widely respected tool that may help you understand and correct a lack of personal boundaries. It might help you leave your SO's pain with them, and take responsibility for your own feelings.

In All Our Affairs - Making Crises Work for You - by Al-Anon - When you are really ready to face your true feelings about your relationship, I highly recommend this book. Don't be distracted by alcoholism, if your SO is not. It's the behavior and the feelings that count, and this book is right on target. This book made me cry more than anything else I read.

Struggle for Intimacy - by Janet Woititz - This book helped me understand my wife and what was happening inside her. It is written for adult children of alcoholics, but guess what? It applies to anyone who grew up in a dysfunctional home.

Tao te Ching - translated by Stephen Mitchell - If you have a mind that thrives on abstract thinking, you will find much insight in this ancient Chinese view of the spirit and spirituality. The Tao has been the defining document for my own spirituality. This translation is very readable, and easy to apply.

There are many, *many* books that can help you in your recovery. These are the ones that most helped me. Read everything that works for you.

The Road Less Traveled

This book, by M Scott Peck, helped me tremendously. Since I know not everyone has time to read everything, I thought I would offer some of my own pointers into this work.

If you only have limited time, I would suggest you focus on the sections on love and grace.

Love: Most nons are very concerned about love. Peck can help you see better how much you're getting, what kind you're giving, whether they are in balance. I would suggest the following subsections in the section on love:

- *Love Defined*

- *Love is not a Feeling*

- *The Risk of Independence*

- *The Risk of Commitment*

- *The Risk of Confrontation*

- *Love is Disciplined*
  and especially for nons:

- *Love is Separateness*

If you are in love with your partner, meaning you long to be with her, feel incomplete without her, fear losing her, and such, I would also suggest you read these subsections:

- *Falling in "Love"*

- *The Myth of Romantic Love*
  and I also think you should think hard about this section:

- *More about Ego Boundaries*

Nons need this kind of definition of love. We need to think and measure our relationships. Most of us give real love, but get very little. We really have to step back and ask how this fits with what we want in life. Most of us are living in emotional deprivation. I know I have been for a long time. Peck, more than anything, convinced me not just that I deserved better, but that I *needed* better. I hope you'll spend some thought time with the concept Peck describes.

Grace: The subjects I'd recommend out of this section may not fit this heading so well. The concepts that jump out at me here are the power of our unconscious mind, the guidance it offers us (and in fact demands we follow), and what happens when we do and don't follow that guidance. Don't be offended by my simple mind here, but frankly this section is the only definition of GOD that I have ever found that *works* for me. And Peck argues that it is really just another way of stating the beliefs of Christianity and other religions. But for me, this was a revelation that *truth* has always been right there, within me, for me to tap. Now I am starting to tap into that truth, and finding it very powerful.

So enough sermonizing. Peck does it much better. I suggest these subsections:

- The Miracle of the Unconscious

- The Definition of Grace

- Entropy and Original Sin

- The Evolution of Consciousness

- The Nature of Power

For those of you who might wonder how I can write all this, wonder where these thoughts come from, wonder where the energy to stitch all this together comes from, read the last section carefully. For honestly, I have no idea how I could possibly do this.

Liberation: Peck's words are powerful. The concepts are pure and true. Not all these things are easy to accept - the emotion of fear might prevent us from allowing the concepts to work through our minds. But exposing ourselves to them can only help. I hope you spend some time with this book and benefit from it as much as I have.

My Recovery Library

Wow. I didn't realize how much I had read. I've read and in some cases studied all of these in my recovery process.

BPD:

- Stop Walking on Eggshells, Paul Mason and Randi Kreger

- I Hate You - Don't Leave Me, Jerold Kreisman and Hal Straus

- Understanding the Borderline Mother, Christine Ann Lawson

Love and Relationships:

- Getting the Love You Want, Harville Hendrix

- Keeping the Love You Find, Harville Hendrix

- Open Marriage, O'Neil and O'Neil

Psychology and Therapy:

- The Symbolic Quest - Basic Concepts of Analytical Psychology, Edward Whitmont (caution - this one is heavy reading)

- Talk is Not Enough - How Psychotherapy Really Works, Willard Gaylin

Divorce:

- Mom's House, Dad's House, Isolina Ricci

Chapter 10
Resources

- The Smart Divorce, Susan Goldstein and Valerie Colb

- Love and Loathing, Randi Kreger and Kim Williams

- Winning the Divorce War, Ronald Sharp

- Divorce Rules for Men, Martin Shenkman and Michael Hamilton

Custody:

- Children of Divorce - A Developmental Approach to Residence and Visitation, Mitchell Baris and Carla Garrity

- The Custody Solutions Sourcebook, Jann Blackstone-Ford

- Non-BP Custody CD, Randi Kreger, Ken Lewis, and Paul Shirley

- Child-Centered Residential Schedules, Spokane (WA) Co Bar Assoc

- Fighting for Your Children - A Father's Guide to Custody, John Steinbreder and Richard Kent

Spirituality:

- The Tao te Ching, translated by Peter Mitchell

- The Way of Life, R. Blakely

- The Road Less Traveled, M. Scott Peck

- Further Along The Road Less Traveled, M. Scott Peck

- Wherever You Go, There You Are - Mindfulness Meditation in Everyday Life, Jon Kabat-Zinn

- The Miracle of Mindfulness - An Introduction to the Practice of Meditation, Thich Nhat Hanh

- The Holy Bible- The New Living Translation (I did not read this, but have studied it a little...)

Addiction:

- In Search of... Intimacy, Janet Woititz

- Under the Influence, James Robert Milam and Katherine Ketcham

Codependence and 12 Step Programs

- In All Our Affairs - Making Crises Work for You, Al-Anon Press

- How Al-Anon Works for Families and Friends of Alcoholics, Al-Anon Press

- The Dilemma of the Alcoholic Marriage, Al-Anon Press

- Living With Sobriety, Al-Anon Press

Sports Psychology and Physiology:

- Complete Guide to Sports Nutrition, Monique Ryan

- Mastering Your Inner Game, David Kauss

- In Pursuit of Excellence, Terry Orlick

In addition, I participated in:

- Family Counseling - outpatient alcohol rehab

- Family counseling - inpatient rehab

- Al-Anon Family Groups - for about four months,

  and heaven forbid, I even worked with a

- PhD psychologist in individual therapy for 18 months.

No wonder my head hurts.

Stop Walking on Eggshells

This is a classic work on living with someone with BPD. Together with this book and *Meaning from Madness*, give you the best guidance on dealing with this difficult situation. http://bpdcentral.com/

Web Links

There are *so* many resources on the internet. Here are some that have helped me. I can't assure you they're technically accurate, but they have offered me insight. Sites change. If these links don't work, try Google and see what else you can find.

Tears and Healing –
http://tearsandhealing.com/
The online presentation of this work. As of
this writing, this book can be purchased
online here.

BPDCentral –
http://www.bpdcentral.com/
BPDCentral is an important source of
information and direction for non-BPs.

Helen's World of BPD Resources –
http://www.bpdresources.com/
I think Helen has found every link in the
universe relevant to BPD. Use this site when
you don't know where to look for something –
anything – related to BPD.

BiologicalUnhappiness –
http://www.biologicalunhappiness.com/
bpd.htm
Dr. Heller is compassionate and shoots
straight. Read it all, especially his
advice on medications on this page:
http://www.biologicalunhappiness.com/
HowBPD-Y.htm

MentalHelp.Net –
http://mentalhelp.net/

Mental Disorders Index –
http://www.mentalhelp.net/poc/view_index.php
?idx=26
When I need to know what bipolar disorder, or
narcissism is, I go here. Includes borderline
personality disorder diagnosis on this page:

www.mentalhelp.net/poc/view_doc.php?type=
doc&id=517

BPD411 –
http://bpd411.org/
Support and information for non-BPs

The DSM IV –
http://www.psychpage.com/learning/library/co
unseling/dsm4.html
The official diagnostic definition of mental
health diseases.

Verbal Abuse Pages –
http://www.drirene.com/verbalabuse.htm
We all need this. It hurts to read but it must be
done.

AL-ANON and ALATEEN -
http://www.al-anon.alateen.org/
Consider this, even if your SO is not alcoholic.

Borderline and Beyond -
http://laurapaxton.com/
A Program of Recovery from Borderline
Personality Disorder (BPD) by Laura Paxton -
Might be useful to you or your SO.

Borderline Pathology and Treatment -
http://www.toddlertime.com/dx/borderline/inde
x.htm
A site called ToddlerTime

Borderline Personality Disorder Sanctuary -
http://www.mhsanctuary.com/borderline/
Some good stuff

SoulsSelfHelpCentral -
http://www.soulselfhelp.on.ca/
Click on Borderline Personality - for BPs

NIMH Medications -
http://www.nimh.nih.gov/publicat/medicate.cf
m
Covers the spectrum

Recovery Man -
http://www.recovery-man.com/index.htm
A great personal site - Recovery from
addictions, alcoholism, abusive relationships
and codependency.

Self Injury -
http://www.mirror-mirror.org/selfinj.htm
Thankfully not one of my personal challenges,
but this site might help if it's one of yours.

The Biology of Borderline Personality
Disorder-MHSanctuary
http://www.mhsanctuary.com/borderline/sieve
r.htm

The Good Drug Guide new mood-
brighteners and antidepressants -
http://www.biopsychiatry.com/index.html
A different view on psych meds.

There are many, many others.

Chapter 10
Resources

Glossary

ACOA - Adult Child(ren) of Alcoholics - an adult who grew up in a home with at least one active alcoholic parent.

BP - A person who has Borderline Personality Disorder or behavior characteristic of the disorder. This includes people with lots of problems other than BPD.

BPD - Borderline Personality Disorder - A mental illness, almost always stemming from childhood neglect, mistreatment, or abuse, which leads to adult behavior that changes quickly from normal to bizarre. The best way to tell if your SO has BPD or BPD behavior is to visit the "BPD Characteristics" page on BPDCentral: http://www.bpdcentral.com/resources/basics/indicators.shtml

BPSO - The significant other (SO) of the non who is diagnosed with BPD or has BPD-like behaviors.

Dissociation - A subconscious protection that prevents us from remembering painful experiences.

Dysphoria - Intense, inappropriate anger, sadness, anxiety; an episodic state of extreme distress for the BP and usually the non, too.

Hoovering - A period, usually after a rage or disagreement, where a BP acts in their sweetest, most loving way, trying to "suck" you back in and prevent you from leaving the relationship. From the vacuum cleaner.

NEC - Not Even Close - designates a BP or BP behavior where the person denies they have BPD

NECW - a NEC wife

Non - a non-BP, non-BPD, non-alcoholic, etc; a person in a relationship with someone who has big problems, or who is affected by a past relationship with a someone with big problems.

SO – Significant Other, here usually a BPSO (one suffering from borderline personality disorder or its traits)

Splitting – viewing a person (or object, even) as either idealized or demonized. SOs are "split good" or "split bad", depending on the situation. In some cases, the BP denies ever knowing the SO. I call this being split out of existence.

STBX – soon-to-be-ex, as in divorced.

SWOE - *Stop Walking on Eggshells*, by Paul Mason and Randi Kreger. For many of us, the non bible. If you have to read this description, you need to buy it.

Also by Richard Skerritt:

Meaning from Madness
Understanding the Hidden Patterns that Motivate
Abusers: Narcissists, Borderlines, and Sociopaths
http://dalkeithpress.com/meaningfrommadness/

In Love and Loving It – Or Not!
A Users Guide to Love and Being In-Love
http://dalkeithpress.com/inlove/

The Way of Respect
Ancient Wisdom Adapted for Today
http://dalkeithpress.com/wayofrespect/

and visit
http://dalkeithpress.com/
to look for other new works from Richard
Skerritt.